Ed Cima was born in 1980 in the west country. He currently lives in London with his 2 children, co-parenting with his ex-wife Nikki. He grew up and went to boarding school in Salisbury aged 7. He left school at 16 to follow his dreams. He now owns and works in the infamous E.Scissorhands hair salon in Highgate North London. He's a doting father, an avid tennis player and energetic pioneer.

ED CIMA

ED'S ODYSSEY HOW I MET BUDDHA AND THE ALIENS

AUSTIN MACAULEY PUBLISHERS™
LONDON • CAMBRIDGE • NEW YORK • SHARJAH

Copyright © Ed Cima 2023

The right of Ed Cima to be identified as the author of this work has been asserted by the author in accordance with sections 77 and 78 of the Copyright, Designs and Patents Act 1988.

All rights reserved. No part of this publication may be reproduced, stored in a retrieval system, or transmitted in any form or by any means, electronic, mechanical, photocopying, recording, or otherwise, without the prior permission of the publishers.

Any person who commits any unauthorised act in relation to this publication may be liable for criminal prosecution and civil claims for damages.

The story, the experiences, and the words are the author's alone.

A CIP catalogue record for this title is available from the British Library.

ISBN 9781528996952 (Paperback)
ISBN 9781398488359 (ePub e-book)
ISBN 9781398488342 (Audiobook)

www.austinmacauley.com
First Published 2023
Austin Macauley Publishers Ltd®
1 Canada Square
Canary Wharf
London
E14 5AA

Big thanks to Kiesha Gibbs for helping to edit this book and for all of your support.
Thanks to life for giving me the opportunity to live and experience it.

Chapter 1

It was the perfect night for catching worms. The rain had finally stopped after a day of constant showers. Every time I looked at the sky, I knew that this was going to be the perfect night for my mission. I walked over the dimly lit patch of grass opposite our home, Playfair House. The nearby streetlamp gave just enough light. My senses were heightened, and I could smell the damp air more prominently than ever. I scanned the periphery of the illuminated area. Each blade of grass was sprayed with droplets of rain.

The scene was set. The smattering of clouds floated delicately across the inky black star-laden sky. The clean Wiltshire air would occasionally reveal the milky way. Tonight was one of those nights.

I'd spent the previous weeks watching Go Fishing with John Wilson, voted the 'Greatest Angler of All Time'. So, I felt ready. I was prepared for battle. I crept so slowly and stealthily across the grass, it almost felt as though I was floating. I didn't want one wrong footstep to scare or kill a possible target. My eyes were fixed on the ground, waiting for the first sign of movement. My heart skipped a beat when I finally spotted one. It was just as Wilson had said, "After rain, late at night, you'll find worms basking in the moonlight."

As I crouched down to ready myself, I felt like I had stepped right into Wilson's shoes…and they were big…palpably big. Suddenly, all my learned knowledge and technique left me to be replaced by a barrage of questions. How should I grab it? Firmly? Gently? From what angle and with what grip? Which part of the worm? The tip or the part of its body that's nearest to the ground?

With what was probably not the same technique Wilson

would have used, I reached out to grab it. The moment I touched it, and I mean the absolute first contact of my skin against it, it shot into the ground faster than I thought was possible. It was like a hand recoiling from a scald on a hot plate.

Seconds suddenly felt like minutes, and I knew it was going to be a long night. As a young boy, these worms seemed like mini pythons: some long, some stocky, all of them fast. I probably lost as many worms as I managed to get hold of. Once they got their head and upper body into the ground, they had won. One moment they were there dangling in front of me like a shiny coin and the next they were gone. It was like a delicate game of tug-of-war. I had to be patient yet quick, delicate but firm.

The battle of the wrigglers was intense but successful. My lessons from Wilson had been worth it. I had the best collection of worms I had ever seen, if but only a few. I felt a tinge of sadness knowing they would be impaled on my fishing hook the next day. But they were a necessary sacrifice in the pursuit of my ultimate goal. Trout. Or any other fish that would take my bait and honour me with a fight.

My bucket of wet newspaper was waiting inside at home for me and my worms. Satisfied with my spoils, I decided to head in. I looked up for what should have been a brief moment before I went inside; however, I couldn't look away. I felt so drawn to the sky. It was beautiful. The milky way looked like a light brush stroke of white paint dotted with luminous white spots. It was so vivid against the dark black sky. I was spellbound by the enormity of it all. Suddenly, the light from the stars became brighter. Everything was silent. It was just me, my worms and the billions of stars and galaxies. Then it happened.

I remember looking up at the stars and wondering what forces were at play and questioning how everything managed to work. I could imagine the planets and stars, like the various cogs in a watch moving together in perfect synchronicity. Then suddenly, I was outside of my body, looking at myself from about two metres behind and two metres above. I saw myself standing there on a spinning earth with all the other stars and planets spinning, rotating, and orbiting in perfect harmony and timing.

It was a remarkable moment that only lasted a few seconds. I had seen a snapshot of a world that was brighter and lighter in texture and feel than normal life. It was like I was right there and seeing everything in high-definition animation.

It was so beautifully surreal, special, and strange, but in a good way. It's difficult to put into words exactly how it felt. It was just so other-worldly. When I snapped back into my body, I stood there mesmerised for a short time before I returned to the house. I remember walking into the kitchen and putting the worms in the cool dark pantry. I decided not to say anything to mum about what had happened. I simply said goodnight and went to my room. As time went on, I realised how profound this experience had been. I never battled with looking for answers or wanting any kind of explanation. I was happy to just look back on the moment fondly. At the time, however, I moved on quickly. As a young boy, I had more pressing things to do than ponder life's inner workings and meanings; namely get to bed and dream of going to battle with huge fish.

The next morning, I shot out of bed, grabbed everything I needed and headed down to the riverbank. It was a 15-minute brisk walk from Playfair House. I didn't have a licence to fish this stretch of river, so my excitement over catching fish always came with trepidation. Luckily, I knew the river well enough to avoid the spots where I would be more likely to get caught by residents out walking, farmers, and other fishermen. The river Avon is a beautiful river, meandering through lush fields and meadows, carving its way through the Wiltshire countryside. Lots of old bridges and weir pools with sluices, all creating the perfect environment for fish and nature to flourish. I would often return from a fishing expedition with some extremities soaked from having fallen in the river or lake. Sometimes I was lucky, and it would just be a foot that would get submerged somewhere along the way. Other times, it would be a full leg soaking, usually from trying to navigate my way across reed beds, looking for the ideal spot to fish or swim. The hunt for the perfect swim was always a worthwhile and rewarding experience. I would study the river on a map, looking for the right-shaped section. Then, once I was there, I'd stealthily survey the stretch of water, looking for a covert space where I wouldn't be noticed. I'd avoid wearing bright colours and polaroid glasses were a must, but these were often forgotten at home or lost. I began to know the river intimately. I found that where fast water met a feature, such as a rock, fallen tree, or bend in the river, I would often find big fish relaxing in the calmer water, waiting for prey who were looking for shelter out of the current. This was my playground growing up. I often came up short and caught nothing, but it was the experience in nature that always won the day. I can't remember whether my lessons from Wilson had helped me to catch anything that day, but I do know for certain that I would have enjoyed myself.

Up until this point, life had been challenging at times. Mum had been in Germany for two years and I'd missed her a lot. I started to feel more confident, and I was finding my voice a little more. My stammer, which I had struggled with for as long as I could remember speaking, was still there but manageable. Our house was on a great army camp with fantastic facilities, tennis courts and fields to play in, and obviously, numerous weir pools and rivers to explore. I started to love music and dancing when I had a quiet moment to myself. I could get lost in music and thought. My imagination would run away with me, similar to Walter Mitty if you've seen that film. He'd get lost for long periods thinking about everything and nothing. I was the same. My eyes would glaze over, and I was happily gone. I felt as though my relationship with life began from this point. I started to feel less guided and was able to make more of my own decisions, which turned life into a big adventure for me. I began to fall in love with life, and fall hard.

Chapter 2

Four years before I was born, my parents went through the trauma of losing a child to cot death. Her name was Pandora. She was seven months old.

Mum said they knew something was wrong when they looked at the time, and they hadn't woken up yet. Until that morning, Pandora would wake them up early. I often think about Pandora. I wonder what she would have looked like. I think about the type of person she would have been. On her anniversary, I often get emotional thinking about the many 'what ifs'. I still hold onto the memories that mum shared with me of her. I try to make sure her seven months in this world live on by living my life and raising my kids in a way that I believe would have made her proud.

A year or so later after her death, Michael was born. Then, a few years after that, they divorced. I was around three years old. Both my parents remarried; I have no memories of this time. I don't remember my mum and dad together. I just remember everything being a bit disjointed. There were multiple visits and car journeys to and from houses. Sometimes with dad and my brother, but mainly I was with mum.

My step-mum and step-father were both in a difficult position. Step-parents the world over would probably agree how challenging it is coming into a new, ready-made family. I can say that I now have a great relationship with all my parents. We have love and respect for each other, and we continue to grow and bond in a complicated family set-up. But it was tough at times, growing up. It was hard for many reasons. Looking back, I can see that the main problem was there were too many chefs in the kitchen. Dad wanted my brother and me to experience his values and parenting style, as any parent would. My mother and step-father had their style. Everyone's intentions were in the right place, but it did result in a certain amount of internal conflict for me and my brother. The time I spent at dad's was challenging and rewarding. The discipline and rules were different to mum's but, with hindsight, the balance was good.

Coco, our dog, really helped me become more comfortable with our new arrangement. Dad bought her when I was around six years old. I adored her. She was a French Briard. She had a thick coat of black wavy hair, and her eyes were completely hidden. I've no idea how she saw through her mane. She was incredibly clever and agile. I spent many hours curled up asleep, nestling into her body, as if I were one of her pups. I loved sleeping and shutting down, so this was the perfect place. We had an incredible bond. My lovely step-sisters and brother, Amy and Jo and Peter, were never far away and we shared great times together.

I was about nine or ten when Coco's behaviour became aggressive towards Annabelle, who had just been born. I turned up at the house looking forward to a cuddle and runabout with her when I was told that she had been put down. That was a really tough time. It took a long while to be ok with it.

My father was an Oxford-educated military officer. He went on to make the rank of general in the British Army. I've always been very proud of this. I have fond memories of watching him build an MG sports car from scratch. He was often in work overalls, with oil-stained hands.

It was lovely having my big bro around. He's always had my back and we shared many adventures together. Sports, fishing or wild adventures in any woods we could find were our sanctuaries. Our wild sanctuaries now are surfing adventures, anywhere there are beautiful waves in great locations to surf. And along with my other brothers, Harry and Max.

Mum met B after her divorce. He was a helicopter pilot in the Army Air Corps. He's a lovely guy and does a great job of being a step-dad. He has always made me feel very comfortable and he never tried to impose himself on us. I have wonderful memories of driving fast in his golf GTI; it would be a classic car these days.

As a result of my parent's successive marriages, I have two step-sisters, three half-brothers and one half-sister, in addition to my full blood-brother Michael. I remember trying to explain my family structure to people when I was younger, and they would almost always have very confused looks on their faces. I guess now, blended families have become the norm.

When my dad and mum divorced, me and my brother, moved to a little house in Swindon. We would visit dad regularly. Mum was working for Blue Arrow, a big office-type firm in Swindon, doing insurance, I think. She worked hard. Meanwhile, I began to find peace inside my head, daydreaming and sleeping to an unusual extent. I didn't speak much. Maybe that's why I have so much to say now. At that time, everyone was really worried about it, even dad. He was worried I was having absence seizures or something. I wasn't. I just lived in my world and was just taking my time. It was definitely a case of 'catching up when I was ready'. It must have been tough for my mum. Juggling work and being a mum to Michael and me. I never really caused her too much trouble. There was this one time, however, when I took her very precious engagement ring and gave it to a girl at school when I was about six years old. I'm not sure why I did this. But I remember mum going berserk. This was the only time I remember her losing her temper with me. She's an incredibly accepting and loving person. She sees the good wherever possible.

We had some great times together. I particularly liked our swimming sessions in the local pool, or sitting in on her keep fit classes, colouring or playing with something at the back of the class. We went to shows sometimes. As a result of not being able to arrange childcare, I ended up going with her to see the Rocky Horror Show. I have blurred memories of amazing colours and outfits and music. Seeing Cats was also a big moment for me as a child. Mum was even in a show called My Fair Lady. I was so proud to see her on stage.

Mo Harvey was my mum's best mate, which made her like an auntie to me. Mo and her husband Nick had three kids, David, Martin and Lizzie. David was the oldest. Then there was Martin, who was my brother Michael's age. They were best mates. Lizzie, who was my age, was my best mate growing up. David was my protector when Michael and Martin would gang up on me and play fighting went too far. It was never anything serious, just what elder brothers and their mates do to the youngest.

I was very close to all the Harveys. They loved me like I was one of their own.

They became my family, a sanctuary and family unit that was a welcome change to just me and my mum. I would spend lots of time there when mum was at work or needed help, and we socialised a lot with them. They were so noisy and busy, always with so much going on. I loved it at their house.

They were all very talented at sports, dancing and just most things in general, really. The one thing that I loved was how funny they all were. There was always lots of laughter and games and, of course, tears at times. We would all just get stuck in together and have many wonderful adventures in the woods nearby or on holidays in Cornwall together.

I used to love it when Michael and Martin would get on the wrong side of their dad, Nick. He would go crazy. He would go and get the tickler, (a wooden spoon) and proceed to chase Martin around the house with it. When he would eventually catch him he would get to work on the back of his legs. Not furiously, but enough to prove a point. Martin went on to play football for Swindon town youth and then on to become head boy of the Royal Ballet School. This meant Nick would have his work cut out trying to catch him in later years. They offered us great support and friendship and gave me, my brother and my mother real roots in Swindon.

My mum, the Harveys and my beloved grandparents were my closest family. My grandparents, Mimi and Poppa, had an amazing house. It was a beautiful, thatched cottage just outside of Swindon. It was my home from home. It was the place I felt most comfortable. Big gardens, great trees for bows and arrows and, of course, great food cooked by Mimi. They were just so important to me, to all of us, they gave us stability in a seemingly ever-changing, moving family. It's difficult to put into words how big their impact was on me. Mimi died in 2011 and Poppa died in 2021. I miss them both very much. They've imparted such love and strength to us all. They were just very special people. As a child, I'd hear Mimi's voice and just feel so safe and loved.

Poppa was a very successful consultant gynaecologist. He had the honour of delivering Camilla Parker Bowles' babies. Mimi was the matriarch of the family. She was a great cook. Her shepherd's pie still stays with me to this day. She was a Gladstone by birth. So, funnily enough, William Gladstone, the ex-prime minister, is my great, great, great, great, great, great, great, great, great, great uncle. Despite Poppa being very much the main breadwinner, it was Mimi who laid down the rules. She would make Poppa eat with a child's dinner mat sometimes because he would make such a mess. A Thomas the Tank Engine mat, I believe. I remember Poppa would regularly be seen with a Carlsberg Special Brew in his hand. It was one of the stronger lagers. He would justify drinking it by pointing out that printed on the side of the can it said, 'Approved by the Danish court'. He wasn't an alcoholic, but he liked a drink every now and again. He would sip them slowly, making them last longer. Poppa loved his gardening. He had a ride-on lawn mower which we loved being taken on. He was a keen golfer, and he loved to show us all his best tips and techniques. He even put a chipping hole in his garden so we could perfect our chip shots.

For as long as I can remember, we've holidayed in Cornwall. Mimi and Poppa owned a bungalow in a place called Rock. The bungalow, Little Trelyn, became a home from home. We all loved it there. Everybody relaxed and we all formed our relationship with the place, the beaches and the various shops and bakeries. My brother and I knew every rock formation at our favourite beaches. We named all the rock pools at one particular beach. Gully beach was like a big swimming pool being circular in shape. At high tide, it would fill up and become an epic overgrown swimming challenge. High tide was awesome, especially a spring tide coupled with a storm. The Fairy Pool contained all manner of sea creatures: blennies, crabs and everything in between. We spent hours hunched over, peering into the pool, waiting for that elusive blenny to swim out from its hiding place and take our limpet, which would either be delicately balanced in an open net or on the end of a hook. I can't remember who named it the Fairy Pool. I think it was Lizzie Harvey. It earned this name because of the little sea creatures we could see and all the ones we thought we could see. The pool adjacent to the Fairy Pool was named the Magic Pool. Martin named it this, I think. I wasn't that keen on this particular pool. There were way too many dark spots where it was just weeds and goodness knows what. It was much deeper than the Fairy Pool. The fishing spots were less accessible too, so they weren't as much fun for me.

There was another pool we named the Warmy Dormy because it was always so warm. It never lost its water so it did feel a little stagnant at times, but it was lovely all the same. It was very long, 30 metres or so.

Gully was a special place. We named it that because it had no official name and also because it was as though a U-shape section had been cut out of the rocks, forming a long narrow beach with jagged rocks running either side of it out to sea. We named those rocks the Monster Rocks. So many summer days were spent on this beach. Each family we'd meet had its relationship with and name for this place. Cornwall was like that, a place for people to revitalise and recoup.

Evenings were spent playing cricket in the garden, where we honed our batting skills. Martin would perform the splits and other dance moves, much to our amazement and adulation. I have memories of fun BBQs with great food. Lizzie and I would do our best to mine and sweep the adults' wine glasses and I was introduced to the wonder that is a barbequed banana with brandy. Once we got a bit older, we all earned the right to join the adults in The Mariners. It was a rite of passage. This was a pub in Rock, a 20-minute walk away. It was a mecca for anyone above the age of 15. We would drive past there in the evening and the road would be gridlocked with people inebriated and having lots of fun. There were girls everywhere, singing to songs on the jukebox. I couldn't wait to get there. The wall opposite the pub was where you would hang out if you weren't old enough to buy a drink at the bar. I spent two seasons on that wall before plucking up the courage to go in and try my luck. The beach was just to the side, down a slipway. This was where you and a companion would 'go for a walk' if you felt so inclined. Or, in my case, if the stars aligned, a much older woman would take a shine to me and lead the way. It was a place for growing up, acting stupid and getting taught lessons in life, lessons of rejection and humility. As we all got older, it became less intimidating. We were able to go straight into the bar instead of making a beeline for the wall with our caps on hoping no one had seen us arrive, leaning against the wall as if we'd been there all our lives. I remember one evening, I walked in, I must have been about 15. I confidently ordered 'a pint of numbers' (Kronenberg 1664), put a quid in the fruit machine, won a tenner and pulled all in the same evening. At that age, there were different stages of 'making it', and this was one of the many stages I went through and enjoyed immensely.

My brother and I were becoming quite the sportsmen. It was in primary school that I clearly remember one day being able to catch a tennis ball thrown at me at speed at close range by an older boy. That was a turning point in my hand-eye coordination. I could also throw a ball or bean bag much farther than anyone else. This was the sign of sporting life about to start. Sport became a massive part of my life. It has given me many great memories and helped with my confidence.

Mum had her first child with B, my brother Harry, when I was about seven years old. We had only recently moved to Marlborough. It was lovely there. We were still very close to Mimi and Poppa and not too far from the Harveys in Swindon. Everything felt stable. That was until B was posted to Germany and the decision was made that they would all go out there. That meant it was time for me to start boarding school. Salisbury Cathedral. Michael was already there. I wasn't even eight years old, and I was about to leave home. I remember packing everything into a large trunk and off I went. My speech wasn't getting any better, which caused me a lot of frustration. I had no confidence in my voice and would panic when faced with the prospect of reading aloud or joining a conversation with anyone I didn't know anyone intimately, which was pretty much everyone. I was undiagnosed at this point, and facing the prospect of having to struggle in an unfamiliar environment without my mum. It was a tough year. I missed my mum like crazy. I was allowed to go home to dad's every three to four weekends. I wouldn't see Mimi or Poppa a great deal in that year. I was doing my best to settle into life as a school boarder and treat the school as my new home, but I struggled. I went through a stealing phase as soon as mum left. Nothing of any use or real value to me. The headmaster, Mr Blee, knew it was an attention-seeking thing. He was a lovely man. He knew I was struggling with mum leaving so he dealt with me in a very kind and supportive way.

I was eight and doing great things on the rugby, hockey and cricket pitch. Our team was unbeaten in many of the seasons in all three sports. I was captain and fly-half of the rugby team and showed real promise. The scrum-half, George Shepherd, was my best mate. George and I went on together to represent our county, Wiltshire, in hockey and cricket.

I felt like I had emotionally left home, or maybe home had left me. School was now home, and the sports field was my sanctuary. Seeing Poppa on the side of the pitch cheering me on was just wonderful. He was so proud. He too was a keen sportsman and always had great tips and post-match analysis. He barely missed a match. He kept mum's spirit present while she was away in Germany. I missed my overnight stays with them, but sports game visits were good enough for me. I loved nothing more than seeing him on the boundary of a cricket field when I was batting or fielding. After I finished batting, I would sit with him and listen to his commentary whilst he sipped on a G and T or Carlsberg Special Brew.

I didn't have much focus in the classroom. I was becoming increasingly quieter, and I slept a lot. My speech wasn't improving. A crippling fear would come over me and my heart rate would increase, and then no words would come out. It would look like I was gulping for air and my face would do odd movements trying to coax the word out. It was a nightmare that would stay with me for some time. I became incapable of reading in class or partaking in school plays no matter how hard I tried. On the sports pitch, I was fine; my talent did the talking. Dad was worried. I remember him taking me to the hospital to have an EEG. These sticky pads were put on my head, and I was wired up to a machine. I was 'normal'. They sent me for dyslexia testing and that was when I was diagnosed. The diagnosis, however, didn't explain why I was sleeping so much, why I was still bedwetting and why I had issues with speech and general zoning out. Looking back now, I believe I was probably a little depressed, anxious and missing my mum, dad and brother. All at different times and in different ways. But because I excelled at sport, everything was kind of alright. I think if sport hadn't been there, it would have been more challenging.

The school decided I needed extra help, so I was put into extra English classes as I was falling behind. I didn't feel like I struggled with the work, more I just couldn't stop daydreaming. Anything would set me off; my thoughts escalated like a game of word association. It drove my teachers potty. My school reports always read the same, 'Lots of potential, if he applied himself'. Mrs Walker, my teacher, saw me once a week. She was lovely. She smelled of perfume and cigarettes and had this slow, gravelly voice that put me into a trance. I remember her classes so well. I made great progress with my reading and writing, and I feel I owe her a lot. Classes with her were a turning point in my education, I realised I could do it when I tried.

Being on the sports teams and sleeping in dormitories

made it much easier to make friends. This was a godsend as my social inadequacies would have made it very difficult. I always tried to make people feel as relaxed around me as possible. I've never really been a judgemental person. To be honest, I was hard enough on myself, so I didn't feel I was in any position to judge anybody else. I was fine talking amongst my peers. Words beginning with 'D' and 'J' were hard to get out, so I became an expert at word avoidance. When I was put in a controlled environment, or a figure of authority was in front of me that was when I really would struggle; the words just wouldn't come out.

I was told I was to take piano lessons, but after a year, the teacher phoned up during the holidays and said, "Ed's talents lay elsewhere, mainly on the sports pitch. There's no need for him to carry on." That was the best news I'd heard in a long time. Her name was Mrs Oglethorpe, a lovely old lady. Luckily, I didn't have 'Basher Bourlet' as my teacher. She would bring the piano lid down on fingers and hit her students across the knuckles if the scales weren't performed correctly. School discipline in the 80s was very different to how it is now.

I'd been at the Cathedral School for a year and a half when mum became pregnant with Max. They made the decision to leave Germany and come back home. Things still weren't going back to normal though as dad was being posted to Belize for six months. B and mum had been given a posting near Salisbury in a village called Netheravon. This was where I had my first star experience after my war with worms. I was very happy to be there, but by this point, I'd lost that feeling of needing my parents. I just wanted to start experiencing a more balanced, happy life. I was over feeling angsty, tired and shy. Life was good. I was excelling at sport and mum was back.

Boarding school life was becoming very enjoyable. I

was ten years old, I had a great group of mates, and I felt like I had finally found my independence and gained a measure of social confidence. I got carried away with my new confidence and auditioned for a part in the school play. I loved my English teacher, Mary Guiver, and I was top of the class for creative writing. I wrote about the struggles of being in the strange position of having a speech impediment coupled with talent on the sports field: a peculiar mix of adulation from my peers and self-despair.

I loved drama class. Mrs Gulliver gave us carte blanche. I would always team up with one of my best mates, Will James. He was the best actor in the school. He was also someone who had had many encounters with the opposite sex and would regularly tell me about his experiences. It would take me years to be able to speak to girls.

We would improvise as farmers, old-fashioned dignitaries, and all sorts. We were really good and became a kind of double act. We even started to write songs and perform them for our mates. So, when it came to the school play, I felt ready. Ready to perform and show everyone how far I'd come.

Unfortunately, it wasn't my time yet. I stumbled and stuttered over the only two lines I had. I thought it would be fine as they were being delivered to Will. It made no difference; I still messed it up. I was reminded that an unnatural, inorganic situation with the added pressure of expectation and an audience was too much for me. I decided to keep my creative expression to writing and singing.

I was in a choir for a year or two, although I wasn't a chorister. I was still excelling at sports. My trophy cabinet was growing. I won best player awards at rugby, hockey and cricket tournaments. County coaches were starting to notice me. Wiltshire didn't have a rugby team, but my rugby coaches would often pull me to one side and tell me I could go all the way. It was flattering, but I was just having fun. I loved playing fly-half. I didn't change from this position throughout my school rugby career. I thrived on the excitement of controlling the game. I could create and dominate most games in all sports I participated in, including tennis.

I played centre forward throughout my hockey career, scoring the bulk of the goals at school and county levels. I batted number four and was the opening bowler and, later, first change bowler on the cricket pitch. I was a spin bowler, off-break to be exact. In a way, I believe my mental/social blocks countered my sporting achievements, which helped keep me humble. It gave me vulnerability and honesty. I'm not saying I never lied because I did. I would exaggerate and manipulate sometimes. An attention thing I think. But I knew that any inflated thinking or confidence could be wiped out in a second by a teacher asking me to read in class or having to speak in a group or something. Rightly or wrongly, they stopped asking me to do this. They were trying to save my blushes but, ultimately, that probably kept the confidence demons protected.

It was in my final years at Salisbury Cathedral School that, for some reason, I faked an eye test so I would have to wear glasses. I remember going to the opticians after failing the first round of tests with the matron at school. I pretended I couldn't read the final row of letters. At the opticians, the test consisted of a red laser line of some kind, and I had to guess which side of the dark line the red laser was on. I lied and marginally failed the test, thus rendering myself long-sighted. Mission accomplished. I got to choose my glasses. I went for the loudest, brightest pair I could find. They were multi-coloured and, surprisingly, didn't hurt my eyes much. I didn't always wear them because of the slightly magnified skewed vision they gave me, but I did insist on wearing them for the rugby team photo. Why I did this, I don't know. This phase lasted a few months until a guy called Ben Tanner called me four eyes. I felt appalled and knew, in that instance, that fighting wasn't for me, even if I was really angry. A child psychologist would probably have a clearer view of why I felt the need to wear spectacles, but all I knew was that I felt rather special in them.

Unfortunately, I couldn't hang out in English class forever. The history block was a building I detested going to; as were the science, IT and maths blocks. I don't know what it was about these subjects, but I struggled so much. I'm not sure whether it was down to the teachers or just my brain (probably the latter) but either way, because of my sporting achievements, I was pretty much left to my own devices.

Towards the end of my time at school, I started to anticipate adult life. I was only 13. Boarding school had been my home. It went beyond my liking or disliking it there. It was just home: a part of who I was. The Cathedral School was spectacular. It was one of the oldest schools in Europe, steeped in history. I felt very comfortable there, but it was time to move on.

My mum and dad thought it best I try to get into the same school as my step-sister Amy, Kings College Taunton. I was happy about this. Amy and I were pretty close, and the school prospectus looked good. It was very sporty and not too academic, with great-looking grounds, lying on the outskirts of Taunton in Somerset. The only obstacle was the entrance exam, or common entrance as it was known. I went for a sports scholarship. It was called the Hayward and Barrow Scholarship. I went up there for two days of sporting tests. I loved it. After a long journey in the car, we arrived. I fell out of the car and straight into bats, nets or onto the hockey pitch. I'd planned to do my thing and hope they liked me. They did like me. I was offered a Barrow Exhibition, a great recognition of my sporting ability. The full Hayward and Barrow went to a boy called Jonathan Cox who was academic as well. Ironically, he struggled in the sports teams. Unlike everyone else that summer, Jonathan didn't grow.

The summer before I started at King's, we holidayed in Cornwall. It was pivotal in my growing up. I felt the freedom of leaving my prep school. The preparation was over or so the title of prep school would suggest. I was on the up. It felt like such a giant leap. Cornwall had been hot that summer, so my tan was intense. I was already naturally brown-skinned as my dad was dark and I had got it from him. My brother had mum's fair skin. Dad's family originated from the Italian canton of Switzerland. We have an Italian name, Cima. Apparently, if you go to a little town called Dangio in the Swiss mountains and call out our name, people will open their shuttered windows and reply. A romantic story but I've not been yet so can't confirm this. Being dark-skinned at school helped; it was camouflage and a change from the norm. It gave me subtext and mystique. Although Kings was very multicultural so, perhaps, not as much mystique as I had enjoyed elsewhere.

Girls were beginning to take notice of me more. I was the cute dark one who didn't speak much. Unless I was with Lizzie. Her and I were like peas in a pod. Evenings were spent at The Mariners. I was meeting girls, drinking and singing along to the jukebox. There was the occasional beach party which normally consisted of David Harvey playing music from his car. No matter what car he had, he would always have a huge sound system that was ample for the small car parks and sand dunes. It felt a little like the endless summer, only this time the dread of going back to school had left and was replaced by excitement for a new life and adventure at King's College.

It was that summer that I smoked pot for the first time. It was at my friend Scott's house. He lived in a beautiful house in Stocksbridge just outside of Salisbury. It was a mecca for us; relaxed parents who were rarely there and an older brother called Ross who smoked weed. So, of course, we indulged. The first time I smoked it was through a bong. We all did it. I loved it. It was the biggest and most powerful drug experience I'd ever had. It was more vivid, sensual and mind-expanding than I thought it would be. I went back for a second go a few hours later when the trip had subsided, expecting the same result, but that wasn't to be. It was far less intense. It seemed chasing that first ride was something that would become prevalent in later life with seemingly dire consequences.

Getting fitted for the new school uniform was exciting. The uniform was a tweed blazer. They had a great rugby kit. You were given multi-coloured socks if you excelled at sport, and you were awarded your colours. We had to choose a house that we had to stay in. Choosing a house was a big decision. Each house had its vibe: its code and ethos. To choose wrongly would be like getting on a plane thinking you're going to Ibiza and landing in China.

After consulting with Amy, and having a good look around, I chose Tuckwell. Tuckwell was the house furthest from the main school building. It was unpretentious, sporty and good-humoured. The housemaster was called Paddy, a real character from Ireland. He was a rugby man, so we were a good match. He made us feel very welcome with friendly banter. He loved his job. He enjoyed the social aspect and being a sort of father figure or perhaps older brother to the boys in the house. He would, of course, come down on us if we stepped out of line. The thing with Paddy, however, was you could never take his bollockings too seriously. I'm not sure whether it was his accent or his general demeanour, but I never felt any lasting damage, not like other teachers who would leave you traumatised or hating school after a dressing down. Paddy loved his beer and rugby and he cared for us, so we respected him and tried our best to save him the difficult task of getting cross with us.

My first year at King's was a triumphant one. I was popular and independent. I had the respect of the older boys and my peers. I traversed between social groups seamlessly. I liked lots of different characters. I believe, to this day, everyone has something appealing about them, some talent or passion. I enjoyed many different things, so it was natural I had different sets of mates. They rarely mixed, a little like a Venn diagram that never stayed in one place. I hung out with the sports crowd, the music and drama crowd, the pot-smoking/bohemian crowd and, sometimes, the non-conforming geeks. I befriended this guy called Owen Davies, a total social outcast. He was bright, just not in the eyes of the national curriculum. I would spend my break time transfixed, listening to his theory on time travel. We were 13 at the time. Owen always struggled to get to class on time. The dog had always eaten his homework. I often wonder what became of him.

I played fly-half for the rugby A team, centre forward in the hockey team, and batted number four and was the go-to spin bowler in the cricket team. I achieved great success in all three teams, cementing myself as the most gifted sportsman in the school. I took little notice of this and struggled with the accolade a little. I hadn't grown enough to take such compliments. I avoided such remarks and compliments in general. I now know it's a low self-esteem trait. It was very hard to be right-sized when I had no idea how big or small I should have been.

I had started knocking around with the older boys who smoked pot. I would get caught smoking cigarettes and drinking fairly regularly. The teachers had my number. But I was a nice guy. There was never any malice. I was just often in the wrong place at the wrong time, according to them. So, they found it hard to come down on me. Many of the teachers were also my sports coaches, so they let me get away with that much more.

I remember my first English class. I was so excited because it had been my favourite subject in prep school. I looked forward to developing my storytelling. Much to my disappointment, Mr Rogers and the GCSE curriculum had other ideas. Lessons consisted of reading around the class. We had to read Shakespeare like Richard III and books like Cider with Rosie, which didn't interest me. It was a complete disaster when I was asked to read. I stammered, sweated, and mumbled the words. It was awful; my cover had been blown. People then knew I had issues with reading. Up until that point, I don't believe anyone knew. I had continued with my word avoidance technique, missing out the words I struggled with and starting a sentence with an intro of a word or sound I could get out that would get the ball rolling, like 'Umm' or 'Errrr'. After that lesson, I waited behind and spoke to Mr Rogers, kindly asking him not to ask me to read in class to save my embarrassment. Incredibly, he said, "Okay." It was no surprise that I fell far behind in English and had little to no clue what those books were about. My mind would just drift, dreaming about everything and nothing.

Weekends were a mix of playing sports matches, smoking weed, boozing and girls. It was a dream. The freedom of winning matches, going back to our houses, revelling in the adoration and respect that beating a top school in a nail-biting finish in an epic rugby match, covered in cuts and bruises like a gladiator returning to his pen after battle. That's how it felt, anyway. I'd jump in the bath, and drink cans of beer as it was the safest place to do so. Then, I'd head over to the main school where the girls' houses were. It was a great time.

By the second year, when I was about 14 or 15 years old, I got selected to play for the school first hockey team. This was big. I was playing with 18-year-olds and I held my own. In the cricket season the following year, I was playing for the first team cricket side. It was now official, I was recognized as the best sportsman in a sports school. New respect from the teachers, girls and my peers followed but it was lost on me, I was oblivious to it. I still had my insecurities and I just cruised through, taking it all in and not focusing on any one thing for too long. I wasn't arrogant or big-headed. After all, I still stammered.

I started knocking around with the boys in the years above me more and more. I was playing in the same teams as them, so I was comfortable. I was smoking more dope and just scraping by academically. I was in my third year now and we were afforded more freedom than some of us could handle. Our timetables were whittled down to our chosen GCSE subjects and teachers seemed to only care if we cared. They didn't want to waste their time on students that didn't give a shit when other students needed the attention. Plus, I was doing the business on the sports field, winning the school matches.

My mock GCSEs were a total flop. I got Es and Fs. I just wasn't bothered. I had a gut feeling my path would take a different route than my peers.

Even though I was in my third year at King's, it was called the fifth year for some reason. I was 15 or 16 years old when it happened. I can't remember all the minor details. I just remember feeling like everything was happening in slow motion.

My mate, Jean-Michel, had said jokingly:

"I hope we don't get caught; our exams start tomorrow."

I saw this as a definite 'touch wood' situation so I walked along the wall to the gate where a branch was poking through, reached up, and that's when the gate opened. 'Shit,' I thought. There was Bob, Jean-Michel's housemaster. He'd seen us climbing over the wall and had followed us. All I remember was Bob asking Jean-Michel,

"What's that?"

"A bong," he replied.

My heart sank.

Jean-Michel's A levels were starting the next day, and my first GCSE exam, geography, was also the next day. We were having a smoke and we'd been caught. I kind of went into shock. I was stoned and in shock. Bob, as we called him, told me to go and tell my housemaster what had happened. This was my worst nightmare. How could I tell Paddy? I knew he'd be so disappointed in me. All I kept thinking was, 'Fuck, this was bad'. I walked back to the house like a dead man walking. I didn't make eye contact with anyone. I felt sick. So many hellish scenarios were going through my head. I trembled as I stumbled into Paddy's office and saw his wife and stammered out,

"I need to see Mr Mckegney."

I waited in the office for what felt like a lifetime, but it was probably only a few minutes. When he came into the office, I could tell he already knew. Bob had called ahead. Paddy looked devastated.

"There's nothing I can do for you," he raged. "You fecking idiot, how could you? How can I get you out of this one?"

I said nothing other than I was sorry. I was experiencing an almost out-of-body experience; I just couldn't quite believe this was happening to me. I don't remember what happened that night. All I recall is the next day, after my geography exam, I was called into the headmaster's office. He sat me down and calmly said,

"This is unacceptable. We can't have the other students

thinking this is OK, I'm sorry but we're expelling you."

I felt a calmness flow over me. Finally, I had been put out of my misery. The verdict had been delivered. I could relax a little. Paddy was sitting behind me. He said nothing. Afterwards, I remember him taking me to collect my stuff, sports equipment, my books, etc. I was allowed to finish taking my exams but not stay on the school grounds.

The phone call to my mum was intense. She was shocked and devastated. I kept normal conversation going for a while, then I dropped the bomb. It took a while to sink in, and then the screaming started. Eventually, she calmed down. It only took me a few hours after leaving the headmaster's office to be completely OK with the situation. I was over it and ready to move on with my life. I was excited by what the future might hold. I got a train home that night. It was such a strange feeling knowing that it had all just finished. Only 24 hours earlier I had been in the system. My future had been vaguely mapped out. GCSEs, A levels, university, then some kind of chosen career. But no, a smoke on a bong and it had all changed. Suddenly, there was uncertainty. It felt as though the Earth had started to spin in a different direction. I left without saying goodbye to anyone. I knew my friends would be wondering what had happened to me. Despite the uncertainty, I felt so alive and in charge of my destiny. The winds of life had changed direction and there was no telling where I would end up.

Unfortunately, my parents, (all four of them), didn't share my confidence. Dad gave me one of the biggest bollockings I'd ever had. He was dressed in his colonel's uniform holding typed notes on a piece of paper and he sat me at the opposite end of the table. By the time he had finished with me, I was a blubbering mess. It was tough but, perhaps, necessary.

A few months prior to this, there'd been a careers day.

We'd looked through books outlining the various careers and the qualifications needed for these jobs. I was stumped. The only thing that grabbed me was to be a PE teacher as I had chosen to teach on my community service days. The salary put me off, but also working in school felt a little off as I wasn't too keen on the prospect of 'never leaving school'. I could feel my metaphorical wings starting to grow. Travelling to far-off places started to appeal more and more to me. Hairdressing caught my eye. There were little to no qualifications needed. I could travel with it and the environment would be social and creative. The stigma of being a privately educated straight hairdresser didn't cross my mind. A few days later, a mate of mine's older brother visited him at school. He was a hairdresser in Soho, London. He was a cool guy who wore smart clothes and had great energy. He told me what a laugh it was. Good money, (if you're good) girls and parties. I was sold! Something inside me said, 'Yes!'.

The gods were listening. A couple of months later, having been expelled, I was in the franchise owner Phil Smith's office of his Salisbury branch of Toni & Guy having an interview to be an apprentice. It was a big culture shock. First, the hours were so long, punishingly long. I was chained to those basins shampooing, giving head massage after head massage, making endless cups of tea and basically being a cleaner. But I liked the people I worked with. I fancied pretty much every girl that worked there. They weren't the usual type of people I was used to. They talked differently and dressed differently. They were more open, honest and rude. I came to love it. They liked me. I was quiet and hard-working. Not the usual apprentice that they were used to, and I had a natural gift for head massages. My lunch break was always cut short because someone had requested a shampoo and massage from me.

Phil was a tough guy to work for. He'd shout a lot. If a junior didn't have the correct products waiting for him to finish his client's hair, he'd go crazy in front of the clients. It was embarrassing, but that stuff didn't bother me too much. I was used to getting in line and toeing the line to a point.

I was earning £50 per week for a 50-hour week. Pretty much slave labour, but it was 1996 and I had signed an apprenticeship contract, so they could pay me whatever they wanted. I was learning and felt in the right place. Life at home was cool. I was barely there, working during the week and hanging out with my friends at the weekend. My plan was to get qualified, earn some better money, and then go travelling. India was calling me.

My drug use had increased. Smoking pot and taking Es was my favourite pastime. I revelled in house music on Es. It was an almost spiritual experience, I was so sensitive to the drug. Mixed with my athleticism, I could go for hours on end dancing and enjoying myself, having my emotions awakened on the dance floor. I loved the vibration and emotion in dance music. Somehow, I would manage to get through work on a Saturday with no sleep, have a spliff on my lunch break, and then back on it on Saturday night.

Enzo's was a nightclub; it was legendary. Salisbury was a small place, so I was starting to get well-connected in the small market city. Life became easy. I knew the bar owners, the club owners and the dealers. It wasn't long before I started being the middle-man for pill deals. I befriended a local dealer with great pills and suddenly I was getting them for everyone. B, my step-dad, had bought me a moped. They got sick of ferrying me around. So, at last, I was mobile. Three months after having it I crashed it. I wasn't hurt too badly. I even went into work the next day for fear of letting the team down.

I was two years into Salisbury life, and I knew everyone.

I'd been to Glastonbury, taken magic mushrooms that I'd handpicked, and had relationships with women much older than me, but I'd hit the wall. I was bored. I'd lost contact with all my mates from Kings. Phil was stalling on sending me to London to the academy to finish my training and India seemed a long way off. I was so sick of cleaning and being an underpaid hair salon junior. I was about 16 or 17 years old and was on holiday when things came to a head. I remember sitting in the garden in Rock at Winterbourne Cottage with the Harveys and I was due back at work in a couple of days. I was having a crisis. I was emotional and confused about my direction in life. It was a real wobble. I thought 'maybe I should go back into education and that maybe my dad was right!'. I'd been working my arse off for two years and I wasn't even cutting hair yet.

The Harveys talked me round. They pointed out and reminded me of Martin's story. He'd gone against the grain, turned away from a potential career in football and become a male soloist at the royal ballet. They could see a similar struggle and dilemma. I had talent and knew, deep down, I should be a hairdresser. Working with hair came naturally to me, almost like a sport. I went back to work invigorated. Everyone at the salon was surprised to see me back at work.

The signs I had been giving off before my holiday was that I wasn't coming back. I was unmotivated and uninterested. But all that changed. I cracked on with my training and never missed a model night. I always showed promise and talent at cutting hair and I stepped it up a gear. Within three months, Phil called me into his office and told me I was going to London to finish at the Toni & Guy Academy in Knightsbridge. The winds had changed again, and it felt good. I was on my path.

I stayed with my godmother, Barbie. Barbie lived in a beautiful Fulham town house on Cloncurry Street. It was only a short bus ride to Knightsbridge where the academy was, so it worked out perfectly. I studied at the academy Monday to Friday and went back to Salisbury on Saturdays and worked in the salon. It was a long week, but the buzz of London kept me going. It was great meeting all the other students from all over the country. I was learning my craft and the dream of going travelling was getting closer. There was one incident, however, which nearly scuppered everything. Two months into my training, I was learning scissor over comb, a cutting technique for cutting hair very short, akin to clipper length. It's the hardest technique to learn. It requires absolute precision, dexterity, coordination and lightness of touch coupled with a perfect scissor action. I was attempting it for the first time. As I placed the scissors in front of the comb, which was placed against the gent's head, I began the ballet of moving the comb slowly up and over the contours of the client's nape and up the back of his head, moving the comb slowly away from the head to create an angle, whilst cutting and only moving one blade with my thumb, keeping the other blade absolutely still to create a straight unwavering cutting line. I was supposed to stop just before the back of the head became the crown at the top of the head, but for some reason, I kept going all the way up the back of the head till I reached the crown. I couldn't stop. It was as if my lawnmower was out of control, leading me around the garden. Julie, my teacher, was not happy. The gent was cool. After all, he was getting a free haircut. Julie fixed it, but she told me I wasn't ready for final training and to go back to Phil, tell him what happened and to say that I was kicked off the course. I was mortified. How could she do this? It was my first attempt and I'd been pretty good up until then. At least, I thought so. I went back to Barbie's, packed up my stuff and got on the train back to Salisbury. It was expulsion all over again. When I told Phil, he laughed and said, "Don't be so silly, go back and tell Julie you're staying, I'll be the one who tells you when you're done."

Now, I wasn't Phil's biggest fan, but he surprised me this time. Not only did he not go mad, but he also saved my bacon. I went back to the academy and walked straight into my class. Julie was obviously surprised at me being there and even more surprised when I said I'm staying. I stepped it up a gear and challenged myself. I went for creative cuts that could have ended in disaster. But they didn't. My scissor over comb became perfect and soon I was one of the best on the course. I had rescued myself when I was in the jaws of defeat.

I returned to Salisbury a little taller; I was a qualified hairdresser at last. Now I would get a pay rise and start saving for my trip. But the pay rise never came. Phil was exploiting me again. I'd been back from London for two months, (still earning crap money, about £400 a month) when he walked into the staff room in one of his rages. He knocked a kettle over my arm. The water wasn't hot, more warm, but that was my ticket out of there. I walked out and got a job up the road. He was furious. I got letters from his lawyers asking for the training money back. I put the letters straight in the bin.

I got a job at a salon called Sweeney's. A man called Brian owned it. We became quite close for a while. I liked him. He was blind in one eye, loved house music, we had some fun times. There was a great atmosphere in his shop. Everyone was self-employed and liked having a good time. Most of the money I earned went into going out, drinking and doing drugs. I was 18 years old, and I loved it. I'd often turn up to work with little to no sleep but somehow pulled it off. Brian rescued the odd haircut on occasion. I was newly qualified, so mistakes did happen. I did however manage to get the money together for my trip after a year or two of work. My mate Scott was coming with me. I'd bought a single ticket to

Bombay for January 14th, 2000. What a way to bring in the millennium we thought. We were ready.

Chapter 3

India was seen by many as the mecca for travellers looking for an experience. The place where magic happened, and young adults found and lost themselves in the cultures and colours of a vibrant, spiritually rich country. I was drawn to it like a duck to a pond. The thought of weed growing by the side of the road, cheap living, no rules and of course the parties in Goa was exhilarating. I just knew I was going to have an adventure of a lifetime. We had no real plan. Our aim was just to get to India and get to Om beach in Gokarna and take it from there. However, our first 24 hours were an eye-opener. First, the airport staff at Heathrow almost didn't let me fly because I had a single ticket. It was touch-and-go, but they let me on in the end. When we arrived in Bombay, the heat was oppressive, and the airport was chaotic, to say the least. We saw a group of police taking cash by a doorway for any person arriving with any electrical items, as if collecting money for drugs on a street corner. The smell was musty and curried. There were random guys praying on rugs whilst others begged with the ubiquitous fat police laughing and counting money. There was so much to look at and we hadn't even got through passport control. I changed £100 and got a huge wad of notes back, 6500 rupees. I stuffed them anxiously into my money belt with my back turned convinced someone would see me and rob me. No one robbed me in the airport. It was the car park where we had our first wake-up call. We looked for a cab and got ushered away from the main taxi rank to the car park by two Indians who were very persuasive. One of them put our bags in the boot. And the other one? Well, he lifted his shirt to show a big shiny belt and said, "Police." Scott immediately saw what was going on, grabbed the bags out of the boot and told the two men 'no' in no uncertain terms. We hurried back to the safety of the airport and were camped out by the policemen who were extorting everyone that passed them. We came to the conclusion that we should wait there till it gets light and then try again.

Six hours later, it was the morning. Outside, the airport looked very different. It was beautiful and vibrant. We got into a cab unperturbed by our first attempt and headed to the ironically named hotel Vulgar. Why we headed there, I don't know. It was Scott's older brother Ross's idea. He'd stayed there once. We arrived at a broken-down unkempt hotel with guys selling heroin outside by the needle. By this time, we didn't care, we were there and already having an adventure.

An assault on the senses is what comes to mind when trying to describe India. There were action stations everywhere I looked. Some activity, a process or method was always taking place. Every square inch of space seemed to be in use and if it wasn't, within a few seconds, someone would come along and do something to fill the space. The smells, colours, activity and noise were a chaotic ballet of life unfolding before my very eyes. India was constantly evolving. New methods were replacing old. The space and people were changing and so was the way they did things. One day a barber would be working by himself happily with no apparent lust for expansion. The next day he utilised the space outside his shop and was selling electronics. The demand to accommodate every need was in the air.

I so much enjoyed those first two days of just roaming the streets of Bombay, trying the street food and talking to shopkeepers. India had cast its spell over me. I couldn't wait to head south on the trains to Om beach.

We arrived at Bombay train station, anticipating chaos, long waits and awkward exchanges of pidgin English to ticket sellers. On the contrary, it was smooth sailing. A well-spoken ticket clerk sorted our tickets, and we were on a train within the hour. I sat for hours gazing out of an open door of the train, drinking in the sights of farmers and villages and ancient-looking cattle. This was the magic of Indian railways I'd read about. The people on the train were fascinated by us. Scott, my companion, was a big Norwegian guy and I hadn't turned brown yet, so we stood out. Kids giggled, others stared, but most smiled and offered their kindness in some way. I came to know the Indians as by far the most welcoming of people I had ever met, and I still feel the same today.

Om beach was beautiful. After a long day of travelling, I couldn't have imagined a better place to land. Palm trees hid hammocks and basic accommodation lined golden sands and the tranquil waters of the Indian ocean. There was a murmur of atmospheric music in the background.

I saw a large man on the beach sitting on top of a generator. He was tall and gangly with dreadlocks. I asked him what he was doing. He replied in a thick German accent, "I'm waiting for a fisherman to take me to the island for the party."

I was excited by this. It was perfect. We'd landed on a paradise beach with a party going off on a nearby island. I elected to sleep in my hammock. The mud hut didn't look too inviting. Cockroaches and various rodents shared our living space, so being off the ground seemed a no-brainer to me. However, sleeping in a hammock is no picnic. It took many nights to get the arrangement right. Waking up with cramp as all the blood had drained out of my legs was the norm. The first morning, I wandered down to the beach looking for a fisherman to take me to the party. I found a guy, and after some negotiation, I was off. An hour later we arrived at a scene I thought I could have only dreamt about. People from all over the world dancing on a secluded beach. There were groups sitting, cooking and chatting, whilst others washed in the sea or the natural waterfall that cascaded down the cliffside. I remember there was a tall naked man that looked like Jesus washing himself. It was very cool.

I loved the fact I was by myself with no one else to worry about. No one knew who I was there, but we all had one thing in common: we had all found ourselves on this secluded beach in India dancing and letting go.

I spent all day there dancing and cooling off in the ocean. I met a few travellers and a nice local guy, but I was happy just people-watching and dancing. It was a little overwhelming at times, a little like landing on a different planet. But that was what I had gone there for. I thought I'd better get the last boat back. I took the view that I wasn't prepared to spend the night. I had little money and no spare clothes, and I was getting a little sunburned because I'd put no cream on. When I got back to the beach huts, Scott was eager to hear of my foray into an Indian trance party. I told him how it had gone down and he was a little annoyed he hadn't made the trip, but we knew there would be plenty more opportunities. He looked anxiously at my face and told me to look in the mirror. I was burnt. Especially my nose and my chest. They had gone a deep purple. I spent the next two days monitoring and creaming my affected areas whilst lying in a hammock in the porch area of the entrance to our huts smoking chillums and looking out to sea, daydreaming and basking in ultimate relaxation. Cows would stroll along the beach, peer into the entrance of the beachside accommodation, and then wander on. Occasionally, we'd even see dolphins jumping in the bay.

Om beach was paradise. No one bothered anyone but everyone was social and eager to talk and exchange stories if asked. We spent two weeks on the beach. I could have spent longer. The lure of the beach was too easy, so we moved on, promising to return one day.

Kerala was beautiful, with a quieter, more chilled vibe than the central India we'd come to know. I spent lazy days lying under huge monkey puzzle trees watching local cricket matches. I even managed to participate in a street game I stumbled across whilst out for an evening stroll. The food was so good, I sampled pretty much everything there was to sample. The street food was moreish, as was the super-sweet chai tea. I felt so at home in India. I even looked like a native. I had lost a lot of weight and I was a dark mahogany colour. The diet was the opposite of what I had been consuming for the last 20 years. I was eating bread, but not as I knew it. I wasn't eating any chocolate, no rich puddings or cream, and no ready meals. Just veg and homemade curries and the occasional bowl of Chow Mein.

India was hot. We'd wake up sweating. I took great pleasure in having my evening walk as it got cooler, drinking in the atmosphere and activity. Because I looked Indian, I could move around at ease, not drawing the attention other western travellers did. I had a camera, but I rarely took it out. I'm not keen on photography. For me, taking a picture is living in the past. I like to enjoy the moment and move onto the next experience. I leave the picture-taking to everyone else. Looking back now, I do slightly regret this. After Kerala, we headed north to Goa. We were very excited to go there as we'd heard some great stories. We certainly enjoyed ourselves there. We went to some amazing parties. However, this wasn't the real India we'd come to discover. Hiring motorbikes was fun, neither of us had ever ridden them before, I remember a few occasions my life flashed before my eyes after being run off the road by trucks during perilous journeys to visit neighbouring towns. But, after a few weeks of crashing and then mastering riding motorbikes to attend wild parties in forests and orchards, we moved on.

We pushed on north and had a brief stay in Hampi. The landscape was littered with giant boulders. It was achingly beautiful; so relaxed and chilled. The pace of life almost went backwards, it was so relaxed. On the way back to Goa from Hampi, I had my first experience travelling by sitting on top of a bus. It was incredible, even though I was nearly decapitated by a telephone cable. Someone suddenly shouted:

"DUCK!"

After that, I cautiously drank in the view from a crouched position.

Jaisalmer is stunning. It's a fortress in the middle of the desert. From there we did a camel trek into the desert. We ran out of water on the last day and had to drink from a burst water pipe. Our guides were a father and son team. I forget their names, but they were wonderful cooks. They cooked us these amazing vegetable curries in the sand dunes under the canopy of stars. Camels are tricky beasts to ride but we got the hang of it. I remember approaching the city after nothing but desert for miles. The fortress stood out alone in a beautifully barren landscape.

Pushka was next. A James Bond film had been filmed there and it played in nearly every café. But, the highlight for me was the holy festival. We had no idea it was occurring. The holy festival is a massive paint festival/fight which gets very messy. I remember stumbling along a street with paint in my eyes when an elephant appeared out of the colourful paint smoke. I jumped out of the way only to find myself in a sewer gutter which ran parallel to the roads. I cut my feet, but I wasn't bothered. It was a truly wonderful day, chasing and being chased by Indians throwing and receiving paint all to the backdrop of music and elephants.

We were probably two months in by now. I know I haven't written much but time slows down in India. I spent many days just watching and absorbing the scene in front of me. I would go out for a walk and end up in someone's house, meeting their family and having a meal with them. This is what India is like. They're such welcoming people. Scott and I would often go out on our motorbikes for an adventure and end up in random places with random people staying somewhere because it got too dark to ride home. We avoided the roads at night. By day they were truly terrifying, by night it was a whole new level of panic. The bugs and flies compounded the problem.

It was time to head north. South India was heading towards its summer and the lure of the cooler climate and fabled chilled vibe of the mountains was calling. We landed in Manali after an arduous bus journey. We instantly felt more relaxed when we stepped off the bus. The north Indians look different from the southern Indians. They look more Nepalese, which is unsurprising as Nepal is just over the border. Manali was beautiful. A valley, surrounded by imposing mountains with villages dotted everywhere and wonderfully staggered fields levelled off to fit into the mountain. A guy came up to us and asked if we would like to stay with an Indian family up the mountain. We said 'Yes' without a second thought. Chand, his wife Vidia and their three kids welcomed us after a 20-minute hike up a mountain. It was an amazing, small, farm-type place. Our living quarters, set out from the mountain, overlooked the river and valley and had vultures buzzing around them. We spent many days just looking out in awe at the mountains and river, smoking what felt like all the hash in the world.

The last party we attended was a trance party up a mountain to celebrate a lunar calendar event. The journey up the mountain to the party was epic. It was hypothermic at night. No one told me it would get so cold. I remember sleeping next to a fire genuinely concerned about my wellbeing because it was so cold. I woke up and my trainer had melted on one side because the flames had been too close to it. But by day, the party was very special. I remember dancing in just my sarong, which also doubled up as a towel and blanket. It was just me on a ridge with no one else but a few vultures cruising around.

We were sorry to leave north India. It was beyond stunning. Being there was truly life-changing and affirming for me. It was an experience that was everything and more than I had hoped it would been. The walks through rice paddies, fields and woodland and the sight of ganja growing everywhere made it feel all the more free and other worldly. The colours and smiles and constant work-living cycle was just overwhelming, yet calming.

Scott and I parted company at this point. We agreed to meet up in Nepal a few weeks later although we didn't end up catching up with each other till we were in Thailand six weeks later. We had travelled well together for quite a while by that point. We had spent more time together than we ever had before. We were due a little break from each other. Not that it was becoming a chore or anything. It was quite the opposite. We both just wanted to explore the land by ourselves. So, it was time to go our separate ways.

After a brief stay in Delhi with a few mates I'd met in Goa, I headed to Nepal. The heat that the hot season brought to Delhi was intense. I had to get out. Nepal and the mountains were calling me. I couldn't wait to get there. The coach from Delhi to Nepal was a 12-hour trip. A few hours in, we stopped at a makeshift shop. I raced towards it, eyeing up a bag of crisps that was hanging on a piece of string. The next thing I knew I was falling into a sewer pit that was, somehow, positioned in front of the shop. My foot was cut and bleeding and the bus was just about to leave. Plus, I was covered in poo. I asked the Nepalese girl that I was sitting next to, to get my rucksack so I could change. The driver said it was fine for me to spend the rest of the journey on the roof. I missed out on a potential romantic encounter, but it was extraordinary driving towards the Himalayas with the silhouette of the mountains dominating the night sky. My foot was hanging over the edge of the bus so the air could cool it down and soothe the cuts. Unbeknownst to me, we went through border control without getting my passport stamped. A month later, I had to bribe the police to let me out.

I remember the street before I got on the bus in Senoli on the border of India and Nepal. Half of it was Indian then, at the checkpoint, it became Nepalese. I was tired, hot and so looking forward to Nepal. India was special but I needed out. The crowds, stress, heat and travelling were getting to me. I was filthy and needed a wash and some serious pampering. As we approached the border, I could see the Nepalese side. It was calm, cleaner and just looked so appealing compared to the Indian side, which was typically hectic. It felt like something out of a movie. As I completed the last police check of my passport, I staggered through the gate and a Nepalese guy rushed up to me, took my bags and ushered me to a beautiful little hotel, which sorted me right out: a cold coke, a cigarette and a bath. Kathmandu was busy, but different from an Indian city; it was less colourful. It seemed more ancient. There were temples everywhere. Sadhus were dressed in orange robes. They adorned the steps and pillars of the temples, like cats lounging in a sitting room, some perched up high, others at ground level. They were often smoking some sort of pipe or were sitting in the lotus position. They usually had long dreadlocks or no hair at all. Their beards were often brilliantly white or dyed ginger. In some, you could see the dedication to a simple existence of peace and tranquillity and little spoken communication. Others tried their hardest to sell you weed or other local trinkets. I breezed around with inner confidence. My bartering skills were really good, so I was paying nearly local prices for everything. I looked travel-hardened; lean and strong and a little wiser. I remember thinking India had been such an experience, everything had gone so right in every way. Even when it had gone wrong it had felt right, almost a necessary part of travelling. I could go home now, a new, improved human being. I had experienced and been enriched by witnessing the joy in life, the resilience shown when faced with pain and suffering in tough conditions, joyous faith and religious ways of life. I'd seen westerners and other visitors embrace the culture and people. I had stayed in beautiful locations whilst listening to amazing music and been helped by strangers with no ulterior motive. I'd seen and experienced the real India, and it was something I'd never forget. To be honest, Nepal and Thailand were almost an afterthought. Yes, Pokhara was stunning, and the Himalayas were awesome. The hash was as good as it gets. The people were wonderful, so chilled and giving. But, I was preparing myself for home. I had been away for nearly six months, and I knew more adventures lay ahead. It was time to leave the hammock I'd been lying in for two weeks on the beach in Koh Tao, an island off Thailand, leave the snorkelling, and get back to the UK.

The flight home was interesting. It was a connecting flight. I landed in Paris lying down across four seats smoking a cigarette. The airline was Biman Bangladesh. I eventually touched down in London. I'm not sure what I expected at the airport. My godmother Barbie was there to greet me and take me back to my mum's in Wiltshire. Even though it made sense for Barbie to pick me up because she lived in London and was travelling down to Salisbury, I would have preferred my mum to have been there after such a long and life-changing time away.

I arrived back at mum's in Wiltshire. As I unpacked my trusty rucksack and strung up my hammock on the kiddies' climbing frame, my mind was taken back to Om beach. Two weeks later, after a serendipitous moment, I was off to Spain for my next adventure.

Chapter 4

Five months after arriving in Spain, so much had happened, and I found myself in one of the toughest situations I had ever been in in my life. I l lay there wondering how I had ended up there, sleeping rough on a beach, addicted to smoking heroin and crack. Just how had it come to this?

I had spent all of my money. The sand flies were tormenting me more than the detox from using every day for the last few weeks. The habit had just started. The only thing I craved more than the drugs was my home. My flight was leaving the next morning. I just had to make it through one last night. I attached my rucksack to an up-turned boat and shut my eyes. I woke at some point to find a Spaniard tugging at my bag. I woke with such a startle, wide-eyed and slightly panicked, that it was enough to send him on his way. I fell back to sleep as my mind drifted over the last five months. It had started out exciting. I was going on another adventure. I had been eager to see what the Spanish mountains would bring. Well, they brought and took a lot, but it was worth it.

Dave Jenks was an old chum of mine. He was in his fifties, wafer thin, with chiselled features covered in sinewy muscle. He was an old hippie at heart. I liked him a lot. He had great stories of being on the road with rock bands, smuggling goodness knows what internationally, but, most importantly, he was a loving guy, had an open mind and loved to have a good time. I met him for a pint, and he told me he was off to Spain to renovate a house he'd bought in a village called Jimena de la Fonterra, in the hills of Andalusia. Pirate country, he told me. He asked me if I'd like to join him. I didn't hesitate. Soon, we were at Dover in his Ford Granada packed to the rafters with clothes, jewellery and other tat to sell at the markets on the Costa del Sol as backup. The customs guy took one look at us and told us to hand any weed we had over. We declined. On closer inspection of our car, he realised he'd be there all night trying to unpack it, so he let us through. As we stood at the stern of the ferry smoking a joint looking at the white cliffs disappearing, I knew something momentous was happening. I knew I was in some kind of flow which was allowing me to experience things that I never would have had the foresight to plan for myself. 'How could anyone be this lucky?' I thought. I had only been back from the East for two weeks, and now this. Spanish hills and pirates beckoned.

My first impressions of Spain were great. I was greeted with great tapas and good pot to smoke. The lifestyle was lazy, and I understood why; it was hot, very hot. We made our way up to the hills, into the white villages of Rhonda and Gaucin. I met Dave's friends in a bar. They were either ageing hippies, gangsters or something in between, living there or on the run, evading the UK. However, they all seemed lovely, and they all had great respect for Dave. We could all tell Dave was getting weaker, more doddery, but they accepted it and still looked up to him; or at least gave him the impression they did. He would later fall ill shortly after I left Spain, with thrombosis. Dave's friends were an eclectic bunch. There was Sparky Mark and his wife Sarah, Johnny the Fox, Pedro Pete and a few other similarly nicknamed characters. The house we were staying in was dilapidated but lovely. A big old Spanish villa we could call home. I wasn't sure how long I would be there, but I was going with the flow, absorbing everything. It was really exciting. I had no money, but Dave sorted me out until I started work. Work was tough. It became clear Dave was in no rush to start work on his dilapidated house. It was in a neighbouring village, Jimena, and I had a feeling I wasn't going to see it any time soon. I found work with local builders, sweating it out on building sites and selling Dave's stock at the markets on the weekend. The market was such fun to work at. I was picking up some Spanish. The market punters were a mix of Spanish locals and English expats and tourists. I was selling jewellery, clothes and trinkets. I wore a cool cowboy hat and had Dave's dog by my side. I'd retreat into Johnny the Fox's huge wagon for a drink or to smoke a joint when I needed a break. He'd park up near our pitch and just hang around. He was often hanging around the bars and cafes where Dave and his friends would meet. They knew him and liked him but always kept him at a slight distance. I, however, felt strangely drawn to him. He had a lot of edge. I'd never met anyone like him before. He was kind of soft and vulnerable but behind that was something else. It intrigued me. He had a dodgy free-spirited vibe about him. I also loved his husky dog, Luna. I should have maybe followed everyone else's lead and kept my distance. But, I was still young and impressionable, and wanted to soak up this new world I was in.

I became quite the market trader. I loved it. It was exciting. I was meeting new people from all over Europe. It was so far removed from anything I'd done before. It felt like a beautiful rite of passage for me. After a few months, my Spanish was coming along. I was settled. I'd made good friends with some locals and was being invited out to great parties, dinners and other social events. Dave was enjoying his time drinking and smoking. I was working on building sites in the surrounding mountain villages during the week and working the markets on the weekend. He introduced me to a local gypsy mafia-type guy named Tomat Quan. He was this lean, mahogany-coloured man, with thick black curly hair and piercing gypsy eyes. He had an almost childlike eagerness that I liked. He was very kind and respectful to me. We exchanged our basic language skills with each other, me trying Spanish, and him English. This was where I learned that body language, vibe and general demeanour paid dividends in getting to know people. Tomat had a baby deer in his house. He and his minions were smoking heroin with a deer in the background. It was surreal. I found out later he had found it injured, and had taken it in to rehabilitate it.

We went on a road trip to a village outside of Gibraltar called La Linea, an edgy but beautiful gypsy settlement. The Spanish government created it. They say it was in protest at the Brits in Gibraltar. We went to buy some cocaine for a party. I was very excited by this. I knew that we would get the proper thing here, and I was eager to try it. We took the smugglers' road through hills with Tomat Quan, the gypsy gangster, sitting in between the two front seats with his head popping out the sunroof. It was one of those beautifully surreal moments. It felt like I was in a movie.

That night, Dave and I went to this legendary party in the village of Jimena de la Frontera. Tomat couldn't join us due to turf and territory issues. It was the Feria season, This is where every village in Spain has its party that can last up to a week. This one was rugged and epic, and we danced till the sun came up. Dave lost his car keys, which was a massive problem at the end of the party. Somehow, we found a Guardia Civil officer who had them. This truly was one of those special nights, I'll never forget it. It had everything: great music, amazing atmosphere, and the cocaine didn't disappoint. Dancing with strangers till dawn. I tried things I'd never done before; found myself in situations I'd never dreamt of. I remember dancing with a beautiful Spanish lady. We danced to a kind of Spanish salsa music. She was mesmerising. There was no motivation for a sexual encounter, I was just happy to be there sharing the sunrise and great music with her.

Johnny the Fox was a character. He had a limp from a bad

motorbike accident. He had no hip bone or something like that. On the upside, it made it easy for him to hide stolen bottles of booze down his trousers by his hip where his hip should have been. As a career thief, he exploited this quirk of his anatomy to great effect. Needless to say, being a thief was also how he earned his name. He had a proper gypsy vibe and a mullet hair-do with a very long ponytail at the back. He was a drug addict who stole anything from lifting bottles out of supermarkets to breaking and entering lockups and garages, etc.

I smoked heroin and cocaine for the first time with him on his bus. I'm not gonna lie, I liked it a lot. Not heroin on its own, but the two mixed together. As I drew the pipe nervously to my mouth and inhaled, I could see the bellowing, spiralling smoke go through the neck of the pipe, into my mouth and lungs. Within seconds, I felt a warmth pulsate through my head and body. It was quite remarkable. It was like nothing I'd experienced before. It was bliss, like the ultimate hug. I knew this was the high I was looking for. I started to use with him more regularly. Gradually, Dave got weaker due to illness and was no longer great company. Eventually, he got bored with sponsoring me as his money was running out. I jumped ship and started knocking around with Johnny more. My time with Johnny was weird. A little dark, but ultimately rewarding in the sense that I learned a lot. He did, however, end up stealing from me, giving me a drug habit and had me questioning my moral compass.

I was on a road trip with him one night and he stopped outside someone's house. He asked me to keep a lookout. Without asking why, I did it. Johnny was never really very forthcoming about telling me what he was doing. He knew I wasn't a thief and could have blown or spoiled his plans. He came back a few minutes later, having broken into a garage holding a huge generator. I was initially very uncomfortable about this. My discomfort began to wane the next morning when he sold the generator on the market and I smoked a share of the spoils. After three or four weeks on the road with him, bumming around the Costa del Sol getting high, the rugged shine of Spain was starting to tarnish. I was getting thinner and more one-track-minded in that I started to always be looking for my next high. I was far, far away from the things that made me truly happy. Johnny and I thought it would be a good idea to get a job in Marbella at Toni and Guy's and put my skills to good use. I needed to start earning some more money and the change of scenery was more than needed. We drove through Marbella in his van. It was a big transit van with beds and a kitchen and lovely, interesting, beautifully coloured graffiti on the outside. We immediately got stopped by the Guardia Civil because we stuck out like a sore thumb. Unsurprisingly, we were asked to leave Marbella. We drove off and pulled up around the corner, out of sight. I walked into this posh upper marketplace feeling incredibly nervous. I was walking into a world I once knew but now I was tainted and spoiled slightly through smoking hard drugs and being worn out by Johnny's lifestyle. I nervously walked into the salon, spoke to the manager and made some vague plans to cut a model's hair, to show what I could do, but it never materialised. I knew I could hold my own in any hair salon on this planet, but it just felt weird in that shop. I was thin and had dirty fingers from handling hot drug pipes. Johnny was lurking around the corner, eager for me to bring some money into our set-up. I just felt a million miles away from being salon job ready. So, I aborted this plan and decided to stick to market trading on the weekends. We left Marbella less than a few hours after we arrived. I felt dejected and cheap, like I wasn't good enough for that world. We headed back to Estepona, the neighbouring town, empty-handed.

Soon after this, I remember sitting on a rock in the Spanish hills when a feeling of 'right time, right place' washed over me. It was curious and exciting. I just knew I was meant to be there, and I also knew my next move was to go to London.

Life on the markets was great fun. I'd all but lost contact with Dave towards the end of my time in Spain. Johnny the Fox pretty much had me as his sidekick. I knew I had to get away from him, I knew he wasn't good for me. He was constantly scratching himself from his heroin addiction. He had sores all over his legs and arms. I was also beginning to get the smack itch. I needed to change my situation and fast before I ended up like him or in a Spanish jail. I'd keep an eye out for shop security when he would go into supermarkets and steal booze. I knew I was doing wrong, but it was almost like I would have an out-of-body experience and separate myself from the act. At this point, I was addicted to smoking crack and heroin together. I thought it was a choice and that I just really enjoyed it. But my behaviour and actions said otherwise. Addiction will reason and qualify out-of-character behaviour with such ease and conviction.

My time in Spain wasn't all bad. I went to awesome parties in sand dunes and mountain villages. I'd learned Spanish and learned another trade from working on building sites. I found out I was a good market trader and I'd seen the life of a gypsy, thieving drug addict. Admittedly, I became that to some degree; however, I never lost hope or got too distressed. I believed I was on the path of learning and experience and I don't regret any of it. Obviously, I feel bad about the Spaniards' generator, but that's life and mistakes happen. Luckily, my escape plan materialised when Johnny stole my knife from me. I had it, to use on sites and the markets. It was the last straw. Deep down, I was looking for a reason to leave and this was it. I was gone. I checked into a cheap hotel. I called my mum and begged for a flight home. I had to wait several days for money and flights. I had little money left and had to spend my final days sleeping on the beach dealing with drug withdrawal. My Spanish odyssey was coming to its natural end. Or that's what I thought. I had no idea I would be back in a few months.

I loved being back home. Spain was drifting further away from me each day.

Mum's cooking and being taken care of in general by her was very much needed. I was happy to be away from drugs and everything else. But I had a sense of melancholy. I missed the Spanish mountains and their inhabitants. That place had become my home and I had definitely fallen in love with it, even though I was a bit beaten up towards the end. It was a wild adventure and I felt I wasn't quite done. Whilst on holiday with mum in Cornwall, recovering from and still missing Spain, I persuaded her to fly me back out there, to organise a villa for a holiday. This was my true intention, but I also had another plan. I had designs on smuggling some hash back to England. I booked a single flight to Spain and bought a return flight to Glasgow once I landed in Spain. My thinking was that it was safer this way. A two-day return trip was too obvious to the drugs squad and my quick trip may have raised some suspicion. Looking back on it, the way I did it was far more suspicious. But suffice it to say, I lived to tell the tale. I went back to the village of Gaucin and met up with my old cohorts. I bought 16 ounces of hash, packed half of it into trainers that I hollowed out and the rest I rolled into pellets wrapped in cling film which I planned to swallow. My journey through Malaga airport was reminiscent of the scene in Midnight Express. The character in this film was obviously a smuggler. He wore big glasses, an oversized coat and a look of petrified anxiety all over his being. That's all I could think of. I was nervous. I was convinced I was being watched because I was sweating too much, and my general demeanour was just jittery. I tried to walk as naturally as possible and rushed into the toilets. The police were everywhere with dogs. What was I doing? This wasn't me. I could go to jail here.

I got my pellets out of my bag and coated them in olive oil. I realised these things were less pellet-sized and more fat thumb-sized. It was going to be hard. As I tried to slip them down my throat, I gagged and vomited. It was a hellish situation I had found myself in. I realised I would probably die if I swallowed ten of those large oily cellophaned thumbs of hash. So, I thought it best I just put them in my shoes I was wearing and hope for the best. At this point, my stress levels were high. I had ounces of hash stuffed into my shoes and I had no socks on. After walking past a couple of police officers and a dog, I quickly ducked into a toilet and flushed the contraband down the loo. I took my trainers with hash packed into the cut-out soles and threw them in the bin and vowed never to even think about doing it again. I realised then that life wasn't for me. I think it was just the culmination of being around smugglers and the like for so long. It had rubbed off on me. It had become normal, or so I thought. At that point, I was glad to leave Spain, get to London and find my path.

I was about 22 years old at this time and back at home in Salisbury for a couple of weeks when an ad popped up in the national hairdressing rag. It was for a job in London as a stylist with Toni and Guy in Camden. I applied and got the job. I sorted somewhere to live, a posh squat on Marylebone High Street. It was incredible. A mate had just moved out so there was space. Great timing and what a great place. So many cafes, bars and clubs right on our doorstep. The accommodation was above a greasy spoon. There was hot water and electricity. An old boy called Rory lived upstairs. We didn't see him much. I could walk to work through

Regents Park. It was a special start to London life. I started selling cocaine and also working for local club promoters, which opened up my social life to epic proportions very quickly. OK, it was illegal, but my wages were also borderline illegal. I was working 180–200 hours a month and bringing home £800. This, of course, would set me on a course of self-destruction. But that fuse was going to be a slow burner. At the time, I couldn't see the path I was on.

Chapter 5

London life was an endurance race; work hard, play hard. I loved the London nightlife, the people, and experiencing different groups of friends. I felt somewhat like a chameleon, segueing seamlessly between different social groups. It felt very similar to when I was at school. I didn't attach myself to any one person or group for too long, I guess the traveller in me kept me moving and it wasn't long before I was off again. This time to Morocco.

I'd been in London for around eight months when a job came up with Toni and Guy to work in their new salon in Casablanca. I couldn't wait. I applied and got the job. Head Office told me to rendezvous with a guy named Drew who had already started work there. He was back in London on a short holiday and was about to fly out to Casa. They arranged for me to meet him. He was about 40 or 50, it was difficult to tell. He was very camp and full of pomp and arrogance but with a big heart. I liked him at first. He took me for cocktails in this bar which was in a posh London hotel. He bought me a Storm watch so I 'looked the part', and a plane ticket which was reimbursed when we got there. On my first night in Casablanca, Drew took me out and got me a little pissed. Not the ideal start to my first day.. I woke up with a terrible hangover in 36 degree heat. Waiting at the front desk was Miriam, or Madame Benis as I came to know her. I made it through my first day…. just about.

Drew and I had to share a flat in a part of town called Bourgogne. It was the working-class part of Casa, lively and industrious. He had multiple boyfriends and just seemed to be shagging his way through the Casablanca gay scene. Luckily, he wouldn't bring men back to our flat. If he got caught with a man he would be in real trouble with the authorities, and we had a nosey concierge. He was out on the pull most nights. The night life was pretty good if you had money. Luckily, he did. He liked to flash the cash and seeing as Madame Bennis wasn't paying me, I was glad to tag along. I met some friends and started seeing someone. Veronique was her name. We had some great nights, visiting the beaches and the temples with her generally showing me around town. Casablanca is a lot of fun when you know people. There were very few tourists so it was an authentic working city. Dating Veronique helped me immerse myself in Moroccan life. Drew had paid six months' rent upfront so living costs were sorted, but money was still an issue. I didn't have any savings and was living hand-to-mouth. Casablanca was such an adventure though. A lot of highs, with just as many lows. Working in the salon was tough. The business was struggling. The clients that did come in had such difficult hair. It was like my worst nightmare work-wise. Previously, I was trained to be an expert in the style of hairdressing that was all about the cut and minimal blow drying, creating edgy styles. Casablanca was about big, blow-dried Hollywood hair. The ladies coming in had nearly afro dry hair. It required exceptional blow drying, so it was a steep learning curve for me.

I spent my days waiting for the ever-elusive clients in the shop by day, and by night I was out with friends. We sometimes went out with Drew, until he disappeared off to his favourite bars. When we were out with him, we always had a table. He splashed the cash buying the bottles, and I would have some really fun night's meeting people and dancing. Veronique and I drifted apart and broke up. For a short period, I started seeing an older woman. She was about 40, I think. Inexplicably, I've forgotten her name. However, I was a kept man for a while. I felt a little like Dustin Hoffman in the film The Graduate; a gigolo, trying to survive as my boss wouldn't pay me any wages. I can't say I cared much because I was having such a good time. I genuinely enjoyed hanging out in the cafes after work and speaking my pidgin French with local men over coffee. I loved their outfits, the long dressing gown-style garments. I thought they looked so comfortable. I became distant from Drew. He was often out or away with his boyfriend. I was doing my own thing. I started to hate the long days in the salon. I couldn't wait for the weekends when I would go away with my friends I'd met. I had some lovely experiences in different towns and beachside villages with people I barely knew. But I was amassing debt. Credit card charges were mounting up. I had to go home but I had no idea how I could afford the flight. I couldn't and didn't want to ask mum again. Luckily, after six months of working, Miriam paid me £160 for a month's work, just enough for a single flight home. I snuck out at 5 am, doing my best not to be seen by the concierge or anyone that may have known me. Not that it would have particularly mattered if I had been seen. The whole thing just felt like an escape. I trod carefully and stealthily all the way to the airport, to finish the mission unseen. I told Drew I was leaving but not my boss Miriam. Drew wasn't keen on Miriam, so keeping my secret didn't bother him. I was a little scared of her and she had been so awful with not paying me. I decided I didn't want a confrontation with her. So, rightly or wrongly, (the latter I think), I left without a word.

I moved straight back into the flat in Marylebone. My room was still free. It was back to business as usual. I got my old job back and got back into the groove of London life. After a couple of months, we got served notice on the flat. Once again, change was afoot. Bill, my flat mate, was moving to China and I wasn't sure where to go. Then, a surprising twist of fate occurred whilst at work in Camden. I saw a beautiful husky dog chewing on a raw bone with meat on it outside the salon. I saw the side profile of its owner squatted up against the telephone booth outside the salon. I recognised the hair first. It was Johnny the Fox. Turns out he was from Camden and was back home to avoid the Spanish winter. He was as surprised to see me as I was to see him.

It wasn't long before we were smoking crack in his bus again. I hadn't used any drugs since Spain. I didn't hang out with him much, just long enough so I had the contacts to score. And I was back using it again, albeit sporadically. It was around this time, I first met Jody. She walked into the salon smartly dressed in a long fur-trimmed leather coat, trilby hat and with a Mancunian accent. She was a signed rapper. It was love at first sight. We became friends. I was helping to promote a night at a legendary night club called The Cross. That particular event was called PROLOGUE. It was Jody's birthday so I suggested the club because I could get them in for free. I ended up back at her place with her mates. It was so cool. I loved her crowd. They were a bit older and a lot of fun. Her best mate, Vicky, jumped on me. She took me on a six-week bender: lots of parties. I had a really good time with her. She introduced me to a different way of life. Yes, I'd had girlfriends, but meeting a confident older London girl was a whole new experience. I was a little intimidated but in a good way.

I still needed somewhere to live. I was crashing at a mate's place in Marylebone. Jody was moving house and asked if I wanted to move with her and three other girls into a large house in Camden. I said 'Yes' straight away. The girls were great. Kirsty was a renowned DJ from the nineties. Vanessa was a casino worker and big party girl, and Emily was just so cool and lovely. Jody loved a party and was just so cool, quick-witted and gorgeous. She owned any room she was in. I was so drawn to her. Once I got over the initial attraction, I could relax and be myself. We got closer and closer over time. That first night was so special. We kissed and shared a bed without having sex. I fell completely in love with her. My first true love. From that day forward, we were together, and we didn't spend a night apart for the next few years. Life with Jody was fun. Lots of parties, dancing and great music. I met lots of creative people and had interesting conversations. I grew in confidence through being with her. She was the life and soul of the party.

Over the next two years, I started to use crack on a more regular basis. I managed to keep it a secret and function in all other areas of my life. For the first couple of months, I used probably once or twice a week and thoroughly enjoyed it. But my consumption and need for it only grew.

I started lying to Jody. I was spending all my wages on it, sneaking out in the middle of the night to score, using it at work and with people living off the street as they knew where to score when I couldn't get any. I ended up in alley ways and crack houses in Camden and Kings Cross. The drug got a hold of me and wouldn't let go; I was powerless. The high was just too high. It took me to a place of instant bliss, or so I thought. The high diminished considerably over time but I still chased it. I tried to stop on many occasions, but resistance was futile. I knew nothing of the 12 steps of recovery. I didn't mix with anyone in recovery. Jody eventually found out. She started searching me before I left for work, finding pipes in my socks. Other times she could tell from just looking at me. I looked ill, would stammer and I couldn't get an erection. It was always pretty obvious when I'd been using it. My complexion and eyes would change. I was losing weight rapidly and people at work were starting to notice weirdness in me. After two years, I was done. I couldn't go on like this anymore, I needed help fast. I knew it was time when I started to have physical withdrawal symptoms as well as mental. I ended up in a heap on our flat floor in tears. I was broken. The next day I quit my job. I left Jody, London and, more importantly, crack.

I went back to my mum's and step-dad's home in Salisbury. I was drinking and using recreational drugs occasionally; however, I never even thought about crack. I worked hard for six months in my friend's barbershop to save money. When I had enough saved I flew out to Australia to spend some time with my brother Michael.

I felt like I had dodged a bullet. Yes, I got hooked on crack, but I was out of London, away from that shit. Jody and I were no more but I felt our relationship had run its course. I was too fucked anyway, in retrospect, to hold a relationship down. I hadn't had much contact with Michael over the years, but I was excited to get to Australia and see him. I wanted to learn how to surf. I knew nothing of Australia or its culture. I didn't care. I just needed to get away and regroup.

Chapter 6

I landed in Sydney and couldn't wait to start surfing. After two months of battling with the ocean daily, I finally stood up. Wow, what a feeling! I knew from that day on I'd be a surfer till the day I died. I took so many beatings in the ocean, and a few near-drowning experiences, but I did it. I was strong by this point. I worked in a Sydney suburb called Balmain. It was up-market and a good place to work but something didn't sit right with me in Australia. Yes, there were different cultures there, but I witnessed racist behaviour on quite a few occasions. I personally would get strange looks sometimes. I was very dark at this point. I once got attacked in Balmain. It wasn't racially motivated, more of a case of the wrong place at the wrong time. I got clobbered by some locals around the back of the head with a café chair. A girl I worked with shouted something at them and they came for me. I wasn't knocked out, but I did get stunned and knocked to the floor. Judging by the size of them, I was glad it was one-sided as I don't think I would have fared too well getting tangled up with them. There were some good, fun times. The holiday, however, came to an end after six months with Michael and I having a fight. I think we'd just had enough of each other. Australia was good to me. It had been so long since I had had regular exercise. I think school was probably the last time, discounting the dancing for hours on end most weekends at parties. I was seeing the benefits of what exercise could do to me as a grown man. Thinking about it, it's not surprising I became very muscular. I was always very athletic at school, so there was a good engine under the bonnet. The surf life was wonderful, but I couldn't do it forever. Although hairdressers' wages were very good out there, I knew London was my home, and it was calling me back.

I started back at work in Whetstone, North London. I lived with the manager who had a penchant for cocaine and prostitutes. I kept myself to myself. He had a best mate called Frank who practically lived there as well. I had to get out. By this stage, I knew I had to get my own salon. I was tired of working for other people. I had amassed a lot of experience in many different types of salons. My dad had already expressed interest in setting up a business with me, so I called a meeting with him, and he agreed to give me my inheritance early and finance my salon. I needed managerial experience, so I started looking at and applying for other jobs. I did entertain taking a franchise with the company I was working for, but deep down I wanted my own place. I took a job in Muswell Hill as assistant manager and potential partner, or owner, of a salon called Barron's. David Barron, the owner, was a good guy. He thought he'd had enough but it turned out he wasn't ready to relinquish the controls just yet. In fact, he's still there. But I got the experience I needed to take me to the initial stages of being a manager. I was still terrified of the staff, but I was getting stronger. It was at this point my dad called me up and told me he was moving to London for a new job. He'd left the army as a two-star general: a big achievement. His new role was governor of the Tower of London and Keeper of the Jewel House. This role had always gone to a ranking officer of brigadier or above. When dad showed me my bedroom in the east wing of the house, he opened the door to a beautiful wood-panelled bedroom with a four-poster bed. I knew I'd seen this room before. Years earlier, I'd worked in a hair salon in Amesbury in Wiltshire. I remember thumbing through Hello magazine, and I saw a beautiful room with a four-poster bed with a ghostly figure of a woman, thought to be Anne Boleyn, sitting on the bed. Hello magazine were amazed by the photo and thought it necessary to print as they must have been doing a photoshoot in the house. As I was recalling this memory, dad tells me he has a photo in his office of this room, with a ghostly figure of a woman sitting in the bed. This coincidence blew my mind. How amazing and exciting that the room I had seen years before, would wind up being my bedroom.

I had stayed pretty much in the centre of the West End followed by a weird period in Whetstone, North London and now, finally, I was in the Tower. I met dad at Tower Hill tube station with a bin bag full of clothes. We walked through the main gates, saying 'Hello' to the Beefeaters. Then we arrived at the Queen's house on the common in the centre of the Tower. It was astounding. A huge house that was built by Henry VIII and later used as a prison for Anne Boleyn, Thomas More and, later, Rudolf Hess. During the day, the house was guarded by an armed guard with a bear skin hat. He stood outside the front door, sometimes presenting arms to me, which is a style of salute, as I walked in or out. The house was amazing. It was exactly how you'd imagine a sixteenth-century royal house to look. Huge wooden staircases, priceless ancient art on the wall, vast corridors with wood-panelled walls and, of course, the bell tower, which looks out over London and the River Thames. Thomas More was imprisoned in the lower level of the bell tower, three stories down. My friends couldn't believe it when they came over, it was so far removed from anything any of us had experienced before. Waking up every morning and coming home from work was so exciting. It was like living in a movie set. I'd wander around the Tower sometimes, at night, and just marvel at how lucky I was. The history was palpable. So much had happened there. Almost every room overlooked the Thames. It was like a dream. Taxi drivers never believed me when I said I lived there… and I guess I can understand their trepidation. Asking to be taken there sounded like the start of some elaborate prank. I started asking them to drop me off on Lower Thames Street. If I got in late, there was a secret bell to ring, and a sleepy guard would let me in. Tourists would take pictures of me when I left or entered the house or just look bemused as I stepped over the rope and walked past the armed guard and in through the door. Life was good, surreal but good. It was great seeing more of dad; sharing this very special experience and place with him was something else. I slept in the east wing or west wing, I can't remember which, but it was good to be under the same roof as him. It had been a while.

We had great dinner parties there. The Beefeaters were a fun lot. Most of them, anyway. Because we lived there, we both got to enter the London marathon, which I ran with dad twice. It was special running with him past the Tower, knowing it was our home.

The ravens were extraordinary birds. Huge and petrol-coloured. I would often be walking through the Tower grounds and I'd see the Raven Master clambering over the ramparts trying to coax an escaping raven back to its home. They'd had their wings clipped so escape was futile.

This started a whole new exciting chapter in my life. Finally, my wages were my own. Barron's was paying me the best wage I'd ever had, £100 a day. I had the best of friends in Jordan and Stef and their partners. I met Stef at work, and we became very close. I also became close with his partner, Gem, and their families. Jordan and I met through our mutual friend Gilbert or Gil as we knew him. Jordan and I hit it off instantly. We're best friends to this day. I love both her and Gil so much. We're the three amigos. Their wives, Alice and Jemma, are also my besties. We all had the contacts and the right attitude to enjoy London life, which we did to the max.

I was going off the idea of going into business with David Barron. He was unpredictable and controlling and, when it came to it, unwilling to give up control of his salon. So I was on the lookout for some premises. It cost £35,000 to get everything, including rental deposit and equipment, set up. I felt ready. It was at this time that I met Nikki. Our mutual friend Robert had a party when the Notting Hill carnival was on. A few days later, she, by chance, came into the salon I was working in, in Muswell Hill, where she lived. Our paths seemed bound to cross. We fell in love and eventually moved in together. It was a great time in our lives. We worked hard and played hard and just enjoyed being with each other.

I asked Nikki to marry me one evening in the Tower. She said 'Yes' and dad said we could get married in the Tower. We couldn't believe it. We got married in 2010. It was the most amazing wedding. Nikki was brought down the Thames in the same royal boat that had carried Winston Churchill's body down the river. She was met by my dad in his full general's regalia and a Beefeater escort, which took her through the Tower. The Tower had been closed for a few hours and we had the place to ourselves. We then left it by boat and went down the Thames to Whitehall and our reception in the banqueting room and crypt there. It really couldn't have been better than that. Rubens' paintings on the ceiling and all of our families. It was so special, and I will always be indebted to my dad for organising it and making it available to us. A couple of weeks after our wedding, Nikki went to Japan for work. Crack cocaine hadn't entered my mind for years. However, one evening whilst she was away, I went to some guy's house close to my salon to buy weed and he offered me some. I accepted and that was it. The fire was lit.

For the next year and a half, I was using almost every day. It was a disastrous start to our married life, and I will forever be sorry to Nikki for that. I'd wake up thinking about it. It had got a hold of me. I was functioning OK, but cracks were starting to appear. I was using at work, in between clients. I don't know how I did it. I would ask myself this question regularly and I concluded that I could get away with it due to my talent and the fact I was physically very strong. But this wasn't to last. I spent the business's money on it. It got so bad I had to fold the limited company because I couldn't pay my tax bill. I used in the shop and at home. I was constantly skulking around. I spent my days lying and avoiding, and telling myself everything would be OK. I thought I had a handle on it, but I didn't. I'd stay up all night and creep into bed hoping Nikki wouldn't wake up. I was treading such a fine line, but completely oblivious to it. I was consumed by addiction. My blinkers were on with one goal in mind, and that was to suck on the pipe.

Somehow, for nearly two years, I kept it from everyone. After a while though, there was no hiding it. The weight loss was obvious, and I shared my woes with a couple of mates towards the end. Nikki had no idea until a month or so before I went to rehab. She thought I had an eating disorder, cancer or something else less asinine than crack cocaine. This was a real dark period in my life. However, although I regret the stress, pain and worry I had put everyone through, I do believe it was a necessary part of my journey. Moments of self-reflection brought utter disbelief. I didn't recognise myself. I was finished. I could see death around the corner. I was smoking hundreds of pounds worth of crack in one session, pushing my body to the limits and almost going too far on a few occasions. It was Darren, a friend of mine, who forced me to tell Nikki. The moment I confessed fear washed over me like a wave. But after seeing her face turn from shock to horror and then end with pity for what must have been an expression of my disappointment in myself, words could not describe how grateful I felt at that very instant. She nursed me in the days leading up to rehab as I was in a bad way. My dearest grandfather, Poppa, helped financially. I'd spend 28 days in Harmony Clinic, Cape Town. I chose South Africa because it was cheap and far away, and I saw the value in removing myself completely. Things had gone too far, and I needed drastic change. Not only had my life pretty much become organised around drugs but also myself – the person who used them. I finally understood that the drug was not a part of who I was, but an old thought pattern from my past. I saw rehab as an opportunity for growth. I could change and rebuild the best possible version of myself. There was mental baggage holding me back, I just wasn't sure at the time of exactly what it was. I was eager to get there and throw myself into the programme.

The flight was OK. I had a prescription for diazepam that my GP gave me before leaving. Nikki knew how much help I needed and forced us to go see the doctor. The sight of me detoxing was too much for her. I was met at Cape Town airport by a driver for the rehab centre. I don't remember much apart from a weird phone call home to let them know I had arrived safely. There was no more contact after that.

I was put into the infirmary where I stayed for five nights. Most people were in the infirmary for one to three days. I wanted to join the community, but they said I was really bad at night. I don't remember this. I do remember the strange, concerned looks in the mornings of the others in the next room. People weren't normally allowed to join the classes whilst they were resident in the infirmary because whilst you stayed there, you were on medication: Valium during the day and sleeping tablets at night. I, however, attended classes from the first day. I was ruined, but I didn't want to waste time or Poppa's money. The place was great. There was a huge ostrich in a large enclosure, with pigs, hens, cockerels and goats milling about. They provided us with fun and much-needed contact with something semi-wild and non-human. There were lovely trees and other beautiful flora and fauna, and the weather was so warm. The classes were amazing! We got herded from one prefab building to another. Every class, no matter what the topic of discussion might have been about, provided moments where my mind would be blown away and my level of understanding would reach new heights. It was amazing how much self-control it took just to keep up with everything going on inside but when you're done learning, your head felt lighter than ever before. When your existence becomes consumed by drugs, it's easy to not pay attention to life because most days you don't want anything else except your next hit or fix; however, these workshops taught me to become more thoughtful and less reactive. I learned how to find beauty in the ordinary.

The daily routine started with a 5:30 wake-up call every other morning and 7 on the days in between. The 5:30 crew would wake up, get changed, and get into a minibus and be driven to the local beach. It was stunning. We'd form a circle, hold hands, say a few prayers, then we would walk down the beach and back again. I often used this opportunity to go for a jog. It gave me time to think. I also started going to the gym regularly. Getting my physical health back was one of many steps that led towards getting myself whole again.

On our return we'd eat breakfast and finish in time for counselling to start at 8:30. Other than an hour break for lunch, we would be in a counselling session for the whole day. Each activity would last one to two hours. We'd sometimes do interesting team-building games or funny little tasks, but there was always a greater meaning behind the activity. I remember a great game where everyone bar one person would wear a blindfold and the person without a blindfold would have to guide everyone to a particular point without calling anyone by name. The days were very long and exhausting. Emotionally, I was being put through the wringer, switching from physically and emotionally draining exercises to those that were soul-crushingly difficult. However, every day boosted my strength of character in my struggles. I was learning that that was what life demands from you when it tests your limits: pushing you to step out into uncertainty with nothing but faith for guidance on how best to handle whatever comes next. And coming back even better prepared! Each day I felt I was getting emotionally, physically and spiritually stronger. I started to get noticed as a leader and someone who was having a good recovery. It felt incredible.

I was smoking a lot of cigarettes, but it was cool. I went 24 hours without one to prove a point to one of the counsellors, Steve. He made a big impact on me. Apparently, he was kicked out of his own country for a time, which was why he was in South Africa. I didn't realise someone could be ejected like that. The story was that he was in a meth gang and an absolute nightmare. The Steve I got to know was intimidating and uncompromising but a very good counsellor and a great inspiration to many recovering addicts. I don't see myself as a recovered addict; I'm more like someone who went on a journey of self-discovery. I'm careful not to label myself if possible. I believe we are what we say we are. Lots of people have lots of addictions. If you're fortunate enough to get a chance to face them, go for it and dig deep.

The food at the camp was great, but I couldn't help myself from using jam on my cereal to avoid the limited sugar rule. It was great having regular meals again. The other guys at the camp weren't as enthusiastic about the food as I was. I think I was just happy to be eating regularly. Physically, I was looking so much better. I was loving getting to know the other guys. Some of the stories I heard from them were shocking, both heart-breaking and uplifting. These were guys who had come from the street, from wealth and everything in between. It was fascinating. I had never even heard of some of the drugs that some of them had used, such as the prescription drugs that were smoked through inhalers. Some of the daily tasks I was given to do started with writing down past experiences and answering questions that were in my work folder. It was all a little chaotic for me. I've never been good at organising written stuff, folders, etc. However, I could see the value in it. I put a lot into it as my time went on there. Realising the situation I had got myself into was a tough pill to swallow. I needed a complete reconfiguration. All drugs and alcohol had to be cut out for the foreseeable future. I never wanted to touch crack again, but the thought of not having a beer scared me. I couldn't quite comprehend the 'never again', so the 'one day at a time' saying came into its own. My views on this and addiction would change in the future, but I was happy to go along with whatever they said was needed for a good recovery.

I was introduced to two recovery groups: Narcotics Anonymous (NA) and Alcoholics Anonymous (AA). Both had great meetings set up all around the world. They were a little like a club. AA's 12 steps would become my life shortly after my return from rehab. The counsellors, my new friends and the many challenging moments we had faced all amounted to some great experiences in rehab. There were times when someone would kick off, or there would be some issue with one person that would affect the whole group; we were all sensitive beasts. I learned at the Harmony Clinic that addiction and the behaviours surrounding it were rife in society. Everyone had things they did to change the way they felt, the only difference being I smoked crack and liked it. I was shown fascinating documentaries on how neurological pathways were set in the brain and how we could actually change these and re-school our brains. I was excited by this. I wanted the best recovery possible. Even if I ended up a meditating monk, I didn't care. My competitiveness was returning and this time it was channelled into my recovery. I also didn't want to let my grandfather down.

I had a unique experience in reiki whilst at Harmony. We all had one session each. When the practitioner put his hands on me, I started to feel energy and fizzing and other weird physical feelings. It was an amazing experience. In the end, he moved his hands over the top of me and I could feel pressure all over my body. I had never before felt anything like it. The guy doing it told me that he worked in the city and had had a really bad motorbike crash. In the following months after the crash, his hands started exuding energy and heat. At the time he didn't know what was happening. However, it later transpired that he was activated as a reiki practitioner. He told me I was sensitive to the energies and that my chance at recovery was stronger than most. This was a welcome experience and my first direct contact with the invisible energy that exists. I had another experience when, in a sound healing session with him, he put crystals on me and played this music. I had an out-of-body experience where I got up and put a glass over a candle. Weird, I know! By this stage, the steps were all pointing to me connecting with a higher power, or God as some would say. But for most people, a higher power was easier to conceptualise. I saw it more as mother nature or the universe. I had no concept of spirituality to go to. I did know though, that the existence of this world was a mysteriously magical thing. I was happy to look to the universe or to whoever was ever listening to ask for help. Stillness and being in the moment became a wonderful place to aspire to be. When I achieved it, waves of peace would wash over me.

As my time at the Harmony Clinic went on, my thoughts turned to life back in the UK. How would the new landscape look? How would I be received by friends, family and clients? Is the business OK? I tried not to be distracted by these thoughts as there was nothing I could do about it. All I could do was focus on my recovery and learn as much as I could whilst I was there. The counsellors told me I needed six months in rehab. Initially, there is primary care which lasts 28 days. Then, follows secondary care, which is when you're allowed back into society for visits into town by yourself. But you still sleep in a rehab centre and take classes, etc. There was no way I could stay for six months. How could I? I had a business to save. I was in debt and needed to have lengthy calls with HMRC about overdue tax bills.

They said I'd relapse. I said I wouldn't.

"Get real, Ed," they said. "You have more work to do."

This made me nervous. I didn't get it. I was doing so well; everyone had said so. I needed to get back. I believed wholeheartedly I would be an exception to the rule.

I wasn't.

My journey with the pipe wasn't over yet. At that moment in time I was definitely on top, winning the war so to speak. I didn't realise, however, that my journey of recovery was only just starting.

I made the most of my time at Harmony; I had to. I was changing. I was beginning to feel more confident and physically and mentally stronger. My voice was coming back. I was starting to share more in the classes, question something when I wasn't sure, and I was even funny and outspoken on occasions. Doing this sober, without even a drink, was completely new to me. I was so excited by this new lease of life I was experiencing. The other guys started to see me as a leader. Deep down, I knew I was, but it had been such a long time since I had felt the ability to lead that, at times, I doubted myself. I made some good friends in rehab. I'm not in touch with anyone anymore, but at the time it meant something, and it still does now. There was one guy, I forget his name now, but we bonded. His choice drug was crack, and we'd often share and compare our deprived drug stories. His life story was incredible. He had been homeless with kids, rebuilt himself, made money again, then lost it all and rebuilt it again. When the family conjoin day happened, his day of reckoning arrived. It's a day when families come in and confront their loved ones about their actions in addiction and, basically, have it out with them. It worked like an amazing ballet. The counsellors would bring people in and ask questions as and when they saw fit. My friend ended up feeling the pressure and exploded.

"I use fucking prostitutes when I smoke crack, it's not me but the drug," he screamed.

I mean, it was crazy. There were tears, pushing and shoving, and kids crying. Temperatures ran high. It was a highly emotional day. I found it to be a real learning experience for me as the observer in the outer circle. I saw the pain drug addiction causes families and everyone else around them, for that matter. It was then that I saw the brilliance of the counsellors. Their timing on asking certain questions was something to behold. It was like Jerry Springer on steroids. I learned not to get too close to a person too soon. I don't think everybody that came was ready to go through recovery. They left sooner than expected. Some broke out because they needed to use or simply because they couldn't handle it. We were all working things out. Peeling back the metaphorical onion, seeing what we were made of. For some, it was scary. They didn't like the mirror being held up in front of their faces. Others, including myself, sort of revelled in it. We were ready to change and experience real growth. I was waking up to a truer sense of myself and the reality around me. I'd been in the dark for some years now, but times were changing.

By the end of my 28 days at the Harmony Clinic, I felt ready to go home. I missed Nikki, my family and my friends. I was so nervous and scared about what people were thinking. What did they know? How would I play it? So many questions were spinning around in my head. The counsellors were not happy about me returning to the outside world. They were convinced I wasn't ready. In retrospect, they were right, but I needed to get back. My final group session was very special. Each time someone left, that person would choose someone else to say a few words of encouragement and sum up their stay at Harmony. I chose one of the older guys. His English wasn't great, but the message was inspiring. Now, this guy was totally fucked up when he came in. He was hooked on this prescription drug that was smoked by the street people through a crudely modified inhaler. He once kept everyone up by wailing at the guards like a demented so-and-so all night. This was the early days though and we all had our shit to deal with. He was a changed man. I remember a week before I left, he introduced his family to me on a Sunday when they could visit for an hour or two. His kids were lovely, as was his wife. There was a wonderful ceremony at the end of my stay. We wrote down things that we wanted rid of in our lives, then we ran into the freezing ocean clutching this piece of paper and then letting it go once we were submersed. I heard in my last AA meeting in South Africa that if you get on a plane and tell the air steward that you're 'with Bill' they won't offer you any alcohol. I was terrified about the flight home. It had been drummed into me that alcohol was off the menu for the foreseeable future. The ride to the airport was a nervous one, all I could think of was, '*I want a beer, a nice cold beer*'.

I didn't have a beer at the airport, nor on the flight home.

I didn't have a beer for the following few years.

Nikki picked me up from the airport. My mum paid for us to go straight to Bishopstrow House which was a country club/hotel near Salisbury. It was great. We slept a lot, ate a lot and chatted about everything. It was a strange thing being back in the country. I had had this life-changing experience, yet it still hadn't quite sunk in yet. I was still assimilating it, for want of a better expression. I was so nervous about heading back to London; back to the shop. Crack was starting to enter my mind uninvited. I started to fantasise about my first use-up. This was not good. After everything I'd been through in rehab, and all the money my Poppa had spent. There was so much that should have preoccupied my mind. The business was in a lot of trouble. I also knew that Nicki and my friends could leave me. I didn't care. All I could think about was the first pipe. I remember Nikki driving me to work. I was shaking. It felt like I was drowning in my own sweat. I knew I was in trouble. We pulled up outside my shop. I told Nikki to wait in the car. I walked in for the first time in about six weeks. Luckily, the shop was busy, and I remember noticing my usual clients and the staff were still there. Everything was the same apart from me. I had this disconcerting feeling like I was somewhere in between the familiar and the unknown.

The story we gave everyone was that I had had some sort of episode due to over-tiredness and that I needed a break. Being in the shop brought on such a strong physical and mental reaction. I had used so often there. The memories came back thick and fast. It dawned on me then, that working and recovery were going to be a challenge. Everywhere reminded me of that high that I had chased so desperately. I had to get a meeting quickly. Nikki had been given the information on the 12 steps in an email from the rehab centre, so she knew what I had to do. We sat down and planned out my week's meetings. I have so much love and respect for how much she helped me through the initial period.

I'll never forget my first meeting. It was in Kentish Town on a Friday evening. It was a candlelit meeting with no particular theme other than recovered addicts and using addicts telling stories to try to help others. I remember walking into that meeting feeling excited and scared at the same time. I knew this was where I had to be and where I was going to find recovery. I had been back in the country for nearly a week. My sleep was terrible, and I was always on edge. I was so looking forward to sharing things at the meeting and telling the other guys where I was at. The candlelight was perfect as I couldn't deal with the glare of lights and people's faces. I was at the beginning again. I had been on top of the world in South Africa, leading the groups and speaking out with ease. But back in London, it felt as though I had never been to rehab. I was so sensitive to everything. It was as if I'd forgotten all I'd learned in South Africa. I knew it was in there, but I just couldn't access it yet. I had to find my feet again. I met some wonderful and inspiring people in that first meeting. I wanted what they had: peace, serenity and the ability to smile and laugh with ease. My speech was terrible at the meetings. I struggled to introduce myself.

"Hello, my name is Ed and I'm an addict."

It was a real struggle for me.

The lovely thing about these meetings is everyone has a role. Each one has a tea person, there is a greeter, a setter upper, speakers, etc. You felt like you belonged and that you were needed. Everyone had their issues but was glad to be there, for the most part. As soon as the meeting was over I was inundated with hugs handshakes and welcomes and the question,

"Ed, have you got a sponsor yet?"

This was a decision I didn't want to get wrong. I thought I would bide my time and wait for the right person or some kind of lightning bolt. However, at the end of that first meeting, a guy called Grant came up to me. He had spoken so well during the meeting, and he looked at me with eyes that shone bright and clear. He gave me a look that said, 'Ed, you need help'. I immediately asked him to be my sponsor.

My life consisted of work and meetings. I would do my best to go to a meeting every day although sometimes it just wasn't possible. I would see Grant at some meetings and once a week away from the meetings to start going through the work. The cravings for crack were pretty full-on. Issues I would have throughout the day would lead to me thinking and fantasising about using. Eventually, I did. I didn't tell anyone that I had used, not even my sponsor; which was a big mistake. That kind of secret only festers. You're supposed to tell someone right away otherwise chances are you will carry on using until you decide to tell someone, or they find out. I can't remember the exact situation which caused me to relapse. I do remember, however, that it was not enjoyable. The paranoia that followed the pipe was beginning to overtake me. I would think the police were watching me from outside and that the door would be kicked in at any moment. I ended up hating myself. When a relapse would occur my body had already gone through the experience of using before the drug arrived. It's like I would experience the bodily reactions of using, a tightening of the stomach, raised pulse rate, quickness of breath and loss of appetite. Every time I relapsed I would say to myself that this was the last time. I would promise myself I was going to take my time and enjoy it because it would never happen again. But that was never the case. I would rush it to the point where I was uncomfortable and angry. It was also very expensive. Within a couple of hours, I would spend £200–£300 in just one session.

The dealers were always outside my shop, and I didn't have the tools yet to withstand that level of temptation. The counsellors were right, I should have stayed in South Africa longer.

I needed to get honest. I needed to tell my sponsor and I needed to tell my wife. The devastation and aftermath of a relapse are intense and distressing. It only happened a couple of times, and I knew it was coming to an end. My habits and thinking had changed, but I still had to go a little lower. My sponsor and other friends in the rooms embraced me even more once I told them. I felt such love and support. I will never forget it. The meetings and cocaine anonymous, known as C.A., is a special place where people can and do recover from addictions. I was starting to experience this. Amongst all the confusion and fantasies of using I would see real glimmers of hope and serenity as I did in rehab. Nikki, however, found it very hard to take that I had slipped. I'd been back from rehab for a couple of months, and I was struggling. It was difficult for her to understand the situation I was in. Addiction is hard to fathom unless you experience it. I was trying but the slip-ups hurt and scared her. How could this drug still consume her husband's mind? I shared this in the meeting, and they all said one thing.

"Ed, are you praying? Are you handing over your will to a higher power or mother nature or the universe? Hand it over. Stop trying to run the show. You've proved to yourself that you can't, and you'll die if you continue."

At the time, this seemed a bit extreme, but I've come to realise, people do die from this.

I would often sit or kneel, put my hands together and

repeat:

"I can't do this anymore. Guide me through the day and show me how to be the best possible version of myself."

To some, this may sound a little flaky and insubstantial, but it worked. I don't know how. Maybe it was a trick of the mind. Maybe it was for real. Maybe, I was tapping into a higher power. My whole outlook on recovery started to change. I was feeling confident, and I was excited about the future. My addictive nature was evaporating or at least my destructive addictive tendencies were. I started to value life and sober living above everything else. It filled me with calm and serenity. I believe addictions can be beaten very easily. It's a choice. You just have to start. When those cravings come, do everything in your power to think of something else and to physically do something else. Whether it's reading, praying or some other non-destructive activity, the addictive pang will disappear after minutes. When it returns, we just repeat the process because it always does return in the beginning. But eventually, it does go away, usually after a few weeks. It's just a white-knuckle ride till that day happens. The day you wake up and feel fantastic, happy just to start the day and eager to see what you can give it, makes it all worth it. There are days in the early months that are very tough. Life turns up and cuts through the serenity and good vibes that have been hard fought.

It takes a while to remember the tools that have been given to us. If we are not careful, route one can be straight to the old methods of dealing with problems. Using something.

Something uncanny happened one day whilst I was in the flat. I was struggling one evening, and Nikki was out. Suddenly it was all on me. I needed to use it. Everything in my body was missing crack. I went down on my knees, put my elbows on the sofa and started praying. I used the word 'God' this time. I had no issue with the word; however, it wasn't a word I used often. I may have used it in a tongue-in-cheek way, like 'Please God, no' or something similar, but this time, I was reaching out for help. I said, "God." I said, "Please help me."

That's when it happened, my whole body started vibrating and tingling with an amazing electrical warmth running through it. I was so shocked. I said it again. Once again my body lit up in vibration and blissful vibration and tingling.' I said the word 'God' three more times and three more times. I had the same sensation, slightly less each time but just enough to let me know it wasn't a fluke. This was a wonderful demonstration to me that there was something else out there. It was so physical and conclusive for me. I was in no doubt as to what I had experienced. I didn't tell anyone. How could I? I was in the process of rebuilding myself. My speech wasn't great, and my confidence was low. I thought the last thing people needed to hear was that I had just made contact with a godly energy.

One week later, I had another strange experience. I was sitting in the living room watching television and the doorbell rang. I remember thinking it was weird as I'd never heard that ring before. I went to the door and there was no one there. I looked for the doorbell, but I couldn't see it. We didn't have a doorbell. We never had. My eyes were drawn to the floor. In the flower bed collecting mould was an old doorbell that had once been attached to the door. There were no wires connected to anything, it was just lying in the mud. I picked it up wondering what had just happened. Was this another miracle? Something was going on. I've had many significant coincidences in my life and seen some extraordinary things, but these two events were on a whole new level. At the time, I didn't attach much importance to them at all; in fact, I put them in the back of my mind. I had more pressing things to deal with.

As the weeks went on, the urge to smoke a pipe was getting stronger and stronger. No amount of praying or mystical experiences was able to stop them.

I can't remember how or where I was, but eventually I folded. I scored some drugs and smoked them. It was awful. I can't remember where I was exactly. Probably in a toilet somewhere, miserable, sweating and paranoid.

I told my sponsor in a very emotional state. He told me I had to 'set myself free' by telling Nikki. This is the last thing I wanted to do. It would break her. That's what rehab was for, to stop this shit. Yet, I couldn't, I'd failed, and I had to come clean.

When I told Nicky I had relapsed she went mad. She was so upset she asked me to leave the home.

"Ed, I didn't sign up for this," she said.

I was really hurt by this. In my head, I started to quote the wedding vows: in sickness and in health. But this didn't matter. Nikki was travelling back from working in Spain when I told her I had relapsed. She told me to leave over the phone. I was gone by the time she got back. I packed my bags in a sea of tears and distress and I was on my way. For a long time I resented Nikki for this decision but, in retrospect, it was the right thing to do. I was still not very well and on the edge. I needed my own place where I could focus on myself and my recovery.

I moved into a studio flat in Crouch End after two weeks on my mate's sofa. I remember the cab journey there like it was yesterday. It was during this time that I had to fold my company. I told them that I wasn't very well, and I would struggle to pay my outstanding bills. This was a real low point, a real day of reckoning. I formed a new company, still worked from the same shop and made it work.

In my new place, I bought lots of orchids. I kept the place spotless, almost developing some kind of OCD.

Unfortunately, I haven't kept up. I loved the clean lines and serenity that a near-empty room would give me.

I started sketching the orchids, practised meditation and prayed every morning and throughout the day. I went to at least four or five meetings a week and threw myself into the 12-step programme. I travelled to Grant's place once a week to go through the work and this was when I started to notice a real change in me. Some kind of alchemy was happening. I started to notice the beautiful and simple things in life. The cloud of fear was lifting from me. I avoided parties, pubs and clubs. These activities were so far from my mind. Walking past pubs would leave me feeling a little tense. I had to avert my eyes from the alcohol in shops. I did everything I could to give myself the best possible chance to pick up that 30-day clean keyring.

It was the longest 30 days of my life. I overcame some very strong cravings to the point where I would be praying with tears rolling down my eyes.

It was difficult for my friends to understand. They knew me as happy-go-lucky party Ed. But they knew that I wasn't very well, and I needed to sort myself out and that I would give or do anything required to do so. My language started to change. I started to talk about recovery. This, I'm sure, can be quite frustrating if friends aren't used to it. Suddenly I had more insight into human behaviour, especially addictive behaviour, and a deeper understanding of where it may stem from. More importantly, I knew how to counteract it. I took inspiration from the people in the meetings. I met fascinating characters from all walks of life. Old boys and women that had had huge life traumas and experiences that left me in shock sometimes. To see them fully recovered and helping others was a thing to behold. The wisdom and knowledge that came with strength over adversity were inspiring. I wanted it, I wanted to be that guy who not only beat this but come back stronger than ever before.

I tried my best not to preach this wherever I went, but it was hard as I was starting to walk the walk and talk about recovery. People in the rooms (that's what we call people in the meetings) welcomed my recovery and my attitude. Soon, I was being asked to share my story in the meetings as the main speaker. This is a big deal. Public speaking has never been a comfortable thing for me, certainly not sober anyhow. Yet here I was, holding court and being an inspiration to other people. It was always so touching, after a meeting, to have someone or multiple people come up to me and say they could identify with and took inspiration from my journey. I would always exchange numbers with lots of people, helping them on the end of the phone. When it was needed. Rule one of recovery is to call someone straight away when you're struggling. Just sharing that fact can alleviate so much.

I found that the more recovery-based activities I did, i.e., meeting up with the other people in the fellowship, the stronger my recovery became. I didn't let myself get distracted, I had to focus on getting better. I somehow managed to pay the rent on the flat and rebuild the failing business.

At some point, I started to integrate myself back into my social circles. I never stayed for too long and I managed to stay away from alcohol. People started asking me for help, asking for advice regarding friends or family about a drink or drug problem they had. I always took their number and gave them a call. It seemed that some people didn't have an off button. These people were almost always the sensitive type from birth, and they had suffered some grievance that they had never quite got over. They would harbour a deep-seated resentment about it. It had to be unearthed in catastrophic style by way of drug abuse, mental health, behavioural issues, and the like.

Chapter 7

The 12 steps of AA, I believe, are an absolute godsend. They're a wonderful, manageable and achievable project. They unclutter one's mind and history in a very special way.

It's important to go through the steps with your sponsor. A sponsor is someone who guides you through the 12 steps of AA, a known remedy to addiction of any kind. The support a sponsor gives you can be life-saving.

Before commencing the steps, I had to admit to myself that my life had become unmanageable and I was unable to stop using drugs or alcohol. This was the first step.

The second and third steps were about sharing this with my sponsor, then realising and knowing the all-important fact, that I couldn't beat this by myself. or with help from another human being, I needed to look for help from God or Mother Nature or just power and energy from the universe. Wherever that source was, it needed to be real and credible.

By the time I got to the fourth step, I knew I was going to have to have difficult conversations with people, including my parents, as there were many things from my childhood that I felt needed visiting. I knew I had to lift old plasters, revisit the wounds and heal them. They had left their mark on me and now it was time to deal with them. I was glad I had my sponsor's support through this.

In my experience, the only way to untangle everything is to go back to the beginning of our lives, retrace one's steps and pick through the mess bit by bit, analysing each section of life and correcting and making peace where possible. This is what the fourth step is all about.

It's about identifying where resentments and fears lie and how they got there. I created my list and sat with it for a while. I revisited it another two to three times to make sure I hadn't left anything out. When I felt happy I had included everything, I sat back, looked at the list and thought about what the part I had played in every situation. I could see where I was perhaps over-reacting, being oversensitive, perhaps I wasn't seeing it from the other person's or institution's view. What I learned was, no matter how bad I felt, how badly I thought I was being wronged, I still had a choice on how I reacted to it. This can sound a bit harsh to some. But, to get over something as big as an unresolved resentment from childhood, a complete switch in thinking and mentality has to happen. There needs to be a sort of rewiring of neurological pathways.

The other part of step four was writing down any misdemeanours of a violent or dishonest nature. This, for me, I'm proud to say, wasn't a hard task. Fundamentally, I've always been a loving human being who hated confrontation and just wanted everyone to have a great time.

I always used to be alone. I had hurt Nikki a great deal, shattered her hopes of a normal start to a marriage, so there was and still is much work to do with her. Apart from once stealing money from my ex, Jodi, I used all my own money and never hurt anyone through violence or anything like that. For those that had lived a life of crime and had hurt people, the process of sharing this with their sponsor could sometimes prove to be too much. Some wouldn't reveal the full extent of their past and that hidden secret would fester and unearth itself in some shape or form. Time and time again I would see people go back out using and come back to the meetings more broken than before, only to reveal they hadn't been honest in their step four.

Step five was admitting our stuff to our higher power and another human being. It seems strange admitting these things to a higher power. Speaking into thin air or our heads. But there is some kind of magic that happens in voicing these experiences. You can tell it to a tree and it would still have a positive effect.

Steps seven and eight were about becoming humble and being asked to be relieved of this stuff on a daily basis. I don't just mean asking for this stuff to change once. It's about having these fears permanently removed from my consciousness. It requires constant maintenance, on my knees praying and asking for help when it's needed. And also when it's not. When times are good, it's almost more important to maintain a daily practice of handling my will and looking to give throughout the day instead of taking.

That's the key, to remain rooted and connected in the good times too when it's easier to forget.

This next step worried me.

"Make direct amends to such people wherever possible, except when to do so would injure them or others."

Now, this doesn't mean entirely the way it looks. It can also be interpreted as having difficult conversations and owning truths with someone. Making amends for not being honest and communicating feelings doesn't escape the list. It's a multi-dimensional exercise.

But how could I possibly approach my dad and speak to him about my childhood? I had been deeply unhappy at times, I didn't know how to talk to him about any of this.

Suffice it to say, it didn't go well with dad and my step-mother. I was too aggressive, and I wasn't following the rule of not hurting anyone. I was too honest and vengeful. The truth is, I love them both dearly, but I needed to get stuff out. This process had always been guided by my sponsor. You can imagine how an unguided step nine could be damaging for people.

But I went rogue and decided I didn't need help. I regret this a lot.

Making amends with everyone else seemed a lot easier.

I'd recommend anyone to sit down, write their life story, then think of any resentments you may have, starting from childhood up to the present day, and work out if you need to revisit them and have some thoughtful, respectful conversations with people in a loving constructive way. This is quite a nice place to start if you feel inspired to make changes in your life.

Step ten is all about maintenance and entwining the steps into everyday living. Step 11 involves carrying on with meditation and improving contact with whatever our higher power may be. And finally, step 12 is about passing this message on to anyone who needs it. Upon completing these steps, it is said that one will have a spiritual awakening. This aspect of the steps was never spoken about too much in the meetings. All everyone wanted, including myself, was to stop using and live a happy normal life. I would have no idea that by completing these steps and letting a few years go past, I would have an enormous spiritual awakening that would take me out of the meetings. There was even a sentence in the 12 steps book, which is named, very aptly, The Big Book. It spoke of entering the higher dimensions of existence if the steps were completed properly. This particular sentence in the book was never spoken of or questioned too much. There was also a sentence that referred to nothing being solid, and used the example of a piece of steel not being solid and being just a mass of vibrating electrons. This, again, was looked over as the meeting's knowledge of basic quantum physics wasn't up to scratch. These two strange sentences in the book seemed out of place at first, yet both became a proven reality to me.

The steps were an arduous but fulfilling, life-changing process. It's best to get through them at a good pace in the beginning. This is because, in the early days you're likely to use a drink or drug if you are not doing something else. I found that I needed to go through them a few times over the first two years, and each time I found out something new about myself. This is very common. Each time they're revisited, the onion gets peeled more and more.

By the end, I remember I was walking on air, like an inflated balloon meandering through life, just very content and not being attached to anything or landing anywhere for too long. Just happy to be. It makes sense, retrospectively, that unpicking and sorting a person's past experiences and memories into an organised fashion according to the steps can change one's life in a magnificent way. Everyone noticed the change. I was a better friend, family member, colleague and, more importantly, I was feeling it. Man, was I feeling it! I was walking on air.

I just reacted to everyday situations in such a different way. I don't think I realised how reactive I was until I stopped.

It's like an automatic response and thinking would naturally occur in any given situation. But the steps and this sober life I was living had removed my old natural responses. It was almost as if there was no response: just being in the moment and not thinking too much at all.

Obviously, I would answer when spoken to and I could hold court, so to speak. But I was coming from a far more benign, peaceful place.

Chapter 8

Nearly a year went past, and I was getting ready to collect my twelve-month keyring. I remember walking down the road filled with so much love. I was living and breathing the steps so, by rights, I should've been feeling pretty good about myself. But, suddenly, there was more. I realised I missed Nikki. In an instant, I knew I had to call her and try to get back together with her. I called her later that day and we arranged to meet and chat. She decided to give us another go. I was working the 12 steps and feeling great about life. Nikki and I were trying for a baby. And within six months of my return home, Nikki fell pregnant. It was so special; we both had looked forward to having children our whole lives and now it was happening.

Nikki and I still had our fallouts over nothing in particular. After any fallout, I'm always amazed at how easily the argument started over nothing important. It would set off a chain reaction that could have been halted at multiple points. By one of us, just walking away and ceasing to react, then taking stock and talking sensibly with less emotion. But, of course, hindsight is a wonderful thing.

I was super-relaxed about everything, and Nikki was less laissez-faire about life.

I was beginning to realise we were different in many ways. We saw life through a different lens to each other.

I decided to get back into acting lessons as I saw great value in the process of learning to breathe, listen, speak, tell the truth, and face my fears. This was a wonderful activity for me. When I was acting, I would have to make decisions, get to rehearsals and work as part of a team. It was a great outlet for me to let off steam. I remember getting absolutely destroyed by my acting coach, Zoe Nathenson, but somehow absolutely loving it. The vulnerability I felt was almost like a drug as the reward of getting a scene right and receiving Zoe's praise made the experience special. I would sometimes show flashes of brilliance then the next thing I did would be total rubbish. I never did find that consistency under Zoe's stewardship, not that it was her fault, I just had too many issues. In a room full of 15 actors also doing scenes, one-on-one whilst everyone watched, there was nowhere to hide. I remember nailing my first monologue. It was as if I'd won the lottery. Acting is a funny thing. Whenever I thought I'd done good, the scene was rubbish, and when I thought it was indifferent it was usually good. I have great love and respect for Zoe and her husband, Ryan. It was an emotional journey with them but what I learned more about myself was a far greater prize than any role I got.

Life in the salon was great but very hard. Long days by myself, waiting for clients to come in. I found managing staff very difficult. To be honest, I was scared of them. I would interview people older than me, sometimes more experienced. This is where the acting lessons made a difference. Management to me is a lot like an act. It's not something that I find particularly comfortable or natural. Unless I'm on a sports pitch as captain. I would make seemingly bad choices with staff, and end up with no staff after a year, sometimes even six months. Then I would work alone or with minimal staff and become a little like Basil from Fawlty Towers, running around doing everything. Luckily, I had Anya. She has become a solid friend and permanent member of the team. We worked together in Camden. She came to join me in Highgate. I was very grateful for this as she's an expert with all things hair and a genuinely good mate.

Nikki's bump began to grow. Nikki and I were super-excited and relaxed about the birth. We couldn't wait to be a family. The business was small and ticking along nicely. We weren't flush with cash, but this wasn't a problem. I was in full recovery mode and feeling less and less attached to certain aspects of my past life which used to give me pleasure, like clubbing and parties, etc. If I became a keen runner, I would start to be conscious about what happened to my body. This is not to say I had the perfect diet, but I certainly thought more about the food I ate, the thoughts that I had and the things I did. My friends and family noticed the change in me and I definitely felt a lot better. I would notice that friends, family and clients would come to me with their problems seeking advice. I liked this very much. It felt good to be of use and for me, this was working the 12th step; carrying the message of recovery to people who were struggling.

I always felt great pressure to work the 12th step. So I loved being asked to share my story at meetings in and around London, I even got asked to share my story in a meeting in Pentonville Prison. This was so exciting, I remember feeling sick as I approached the building, I had scored drugs in the past from this area, so I felt a beautiful irony and completion that I was being invited into this place to share and hopefully inspire someone. Although I'd never been to prison it was also a great reminder of what can happen. Going through the building was tense and exhilarating. As I was led through the belly of the prison, it reminded me of a bodily organ: wings all shooting off from its brain; its central nervous system where the main guards' office was. Mission control.

Noises of metal in metal rang through the corridors. Heavy doors opening and shutting acted like a constant beat in this strangest of orchestras. I sat in a room that was in the drug-free wing of the prison. This was a wing that could be used by inmates who wanted to avoid the epidemic of drugs elsewhere.

The prisoners came in and were very welcoming. They

made me feel at ease. I was apprehensive my story would pale into insignificance to them. I was a privately educated, fresh young face to them. They knew I'd never been inside before, but they listened intently and shared realisations and correlations with their own stories. It was an experience I'll never forget.

Back in real life, in the meetings, whenever a newcomer walked into the meetings, he or she would get swamped by the more experienced regulars, those with years of clean time. For some reason, no one ever asked me to sponsor them. I didn't take this to heart too much as there were many people in the meetings that had a lot of experience with the steps and how to teach them. But I know people enjoyed listening to my story. It was quite a rare thing for a crack user to find recovery. Most of the guys and girls in the meetings were cocaine sniffers and drinkers. Every once in a while, a crack addict or heroin addict would walk in, but they wouldn't stay. To be honest, my background was different from theirs. Perhaps this was one of the reasons why I never got asked. Or maybe they could just see that I was preoccupied with work and family. The more I came to know about addiction, the more I realised that it is a state of mind. The drug or the drink, or whatever it is a person is addicted to, is not the problem. It's almost like there is a little button in our brain that for some reason gets stuck and needs to be released.

I don't want to intellectualise addiction too much. Some people reading this may completely disagree, and that's okay. I'm only talking about my experience and my thoughts for whatever they're worth. Someone with greater knowledge, wisdom and experience than me would give a better explanation and remedy to this problem or blessing, as it turned out to be in my case. I say blessing because finally, something made me take ownership of my life, my thoughts and my actions. I was me, but a new, better version of me. I was able to move forward with a clearer mind. I came to understand that I only had to live for the moment, and that life looks after itself.

As a newly recovered person, life seemed very different and precious, and I wanted to enjoy it. In recovery, they were always drumming into us that we should take one day at a time. In the early days, one whole day was too much of a scary thought. So I broke it down to 16 hours as I was asleep for eight. But even this was sometimes too much, so I broke it down to hour by hour, then minute by minute, then, finally, moment to moment. I found this the place to be. What I didn't realise was that I was practising what many of my teachers strongly emphasised, which was 'living in the now'. I was now doing it out of necessity to survive.

Life was going well; our son Woody was nearly here. Nikki came up with the name Woody. I couldn't think of any names. I would think of one and then vocalise it to a client, just to see how it sounded, and seek approval. I was never happy. When Nikki said down the phone, 'I think I like the name Woody' I said, "That's it! That's our boy's name."

I was still going to acting classes when I could, and it wasn't long before I found myself on stage in the lead role in a fringe play. The play was called The Basement Window by Antonio Buero Vallejo. It was such a wonderful experience: so challenging in many ways. I had my stammer to overcome and the fact that I'd never been on stage. My family, friends and clients all came to see me. I was on stage for nearly two hours, laughing, crying and going slightly mad. I was playing a tortured soul who represented socialism in Franco's era.

I remember doing a scene that lasted a few minutes, trying to win my onstage love interest, a few feet from my mum and aunties. It was intense, but I recommend it to anyone. The process alone of acting is an exceptional exercise. It helped heal many insecurities that I had accumulated over the years. After the performance was over, I walked most of the way home through the London night, feeling feelings I'd never felt before. It was very special.

That performance led to me having an audition at the National Theatre to be in a play with Ralph Fiennes. I ended up turning down the recall because it was too close to Woody's birth and Nikki just wasn't into the idea. This was tough to get over. It was an amazing opportunity, but it wasn't to be. For quite some time, I kicked myself about this decision, which is unlike me. But I realised that my time with Woody in those early days and months and years to come was so precious, I wouldn't want to change it for the world. If I had gone into the play, it could have kickstarted an acting career, and that's not what I ever wanted out of it.

I was feeling incredibly happy at this time of my life. Woody's birth was imminent. When he decided to join us, it was on. Nikki knew instantly and she handled it incredibly well. She is a super strong woman who couldn't have done better in pregnancy. She did a great job at getting the flat ready for the new arrival. Everything he needed was there. He was born on a Sunday morning, at about 10 am on June 23rd. It was epic. We were in a private room in the birthing centre at the Whittington Hospital. The whole thing began to be stressful for Woody and we had to go upstairs to the labour ward. But Nikki pulled through and with a final gargantuan effort from both of us, (we were in the birthing chair, so my resistance helped the process a little) he arrived. When they said he had a lot of hair I burst into tears. It was so emotional for Nikki and me, and even one of the nurses was cracking. It was such a special moment that as I write this I'm choking up a little. I found taking him home amazing. It was a level of happiness that I had never experienced before.

Those first few months were so much fun. Yes, it was

tough with not getting much sleep. But the reward of having this little being in our care was out of this world. Woody was such a responsive baby, smiling and engaging pretty much straight away. We would lie on the floor or the bed for hours just messing around, marvelling at each other. I could probably write a whole book on this early experience, but I will move on and fight the urge to indulge too much.

Kids have to be experienced to be understood. That first year of a first child was so beautiful; so exhaustingly beautiful. The funny thing is, I know it was hard, it was painstakingly hard mainly due to the lack of sleep. It really pushed Nikki and me to the edge. But I can't really remember it. All I remember is an amazingly loving extraordinary experience.

It didn't feel like long till Agatha came along and joined us. I'm pretty sure I remember the time she was conceived, just like with Woody. At this point, our relationship was on the rocks, but we were both so happy that we were having a second child, and that it was a girl. It felt like such a blessing. The birth was much quicker this time. I popped over the road to get some pizza, as we'd been there a couple of hours and hadn't eaten. By the time I came back, Nikki was in full labour and Agatha arrived in good time. Nikki did brilliantly again, such a trooper. Massive respect to her.

We were in the process of selling the flat and we had £380,000 to play with. Nikkis' flat sold for nearly twice the price, so we had a good deposit. I thought of Enfield and Nikki was into it. We bought the second property we viewed. It was a great house. Coming from a flat to this was a luxury. The only thing that needed doing was the garden; it was an overgrown concrete jungle. It ended up costing a grand or two. I stuck it on a credit card because I just wanted to get it sorted for the kids. It was like another room in the house. The commute to work wasn't too bad. For a while, I was cycling. It's nine hilly miles: a good workout. I was buzzing about life at this time. I just love having kids. It's difficult to put into words the experience that I've had and I am still having. It just feels like such a privilege.

I know it's not for everyone and I respect and understand that. Agatha was a gorgeous baby. We called her Aggy. She was just so gorgeous. Girls are completely different to boys. She was a wonderful and feisty-natured little soul. I loved playing with them but it was hard keeping up with them. It always has been. I could spend hours rolling around with them, making silly noises and just being on their level. I get quite emotional just thinking about them and when I was playing with them; those little moments that made the experience of life so special. I was so happy but so tired.

Work was going well. I was pleased at this time with the career path I had chosen. My client base was solid, I had pulled the business back from the ashes and I was drink and drug-free. OK, my marriage was not great, but everyone seemed to struggle in their relationships. I couldn't shake off a feeling that it didn't have to be this difficult though, relationships that is. There must be another way, an easier, less fraught and more honest way to be in a relationship. We were getting our highs from our children rather than each other. Teaching our kids to walk and talk was a special thing and that seemed enough at the time. Although, I think we both wanted more. I know I definitely did.

I was still attending meetings, but I was getting bored. They were getting difficult to sit through. They just didn't resonate with me anymore. The tales of woe and misfortune and illegal activity became all too familiar. I knew my time was coming to an end in the meetings, I knew I had outgrown them, or at least moved away from them mentally. Surely that's what Bill, the founder of the 12 steps, would have liked. I later found out that Bill Wilson, the founder of AA, took magic mushrooms to aid his recovery. This method today is widely accepted as a viable course of action to tackle addictions and mental health issues. A means to grow and move on and help others in ways that perhaps I hadn't come across before. I had no idea what was to come but I knew something was. I was more open and taking it moment by moment which, in turn, made me feel like anything and everything was possible. I felt so alive and at peace. People commented on how peaceful and happy I looked. This was great to hear. Even though I was so certain about how I felt, it was still good to have confirmation from others.

It's amazing being free of all alcohol and drugs and praying to the universe or whoever was listening. It lured me into a false sense of security. I had been clean for a couple of years, and I was feeling and looking great. Fatherhood suited me.

After some time, a few years I think, the meditation meeting was the only meeting I regularly attended. It was on a Saturday morning, and we would sit for 30 mins for a guided meditation. I struggled so much with the other meetings that I stopped going. It was in the meditation meeting that something strange happened. The class seemed to last for just a few moments then it was over. It was as if time had been fast-forwarded. I definitely didn't fall asleep; I was fully conscious. This started to happen regularly. Then, one day, I was at home, and I thought of doing a little meditation before work. I sat in the chair in our bedroom, shut my eyes and then it happened.

I shut my eyes and I could hear the kids playing in the corridor. I could see different colours, forming circles and changing shape. It was like I was inside a lava lamp. Reds, oranges, yellows and a little bit of purple. These colours would be coupled with feelings of bliss. Golden lines of lights pulsated through the vista of circular colours. I couldn't believe what I was seeing, it was other-worldly. Like I was in a computer programme, a programme of blissful colours, lights and good feelings. I was observing it with my own eyes, yet my eyes were shut. It was like a TV show that I couldn't look away from. I sat there for as long as I could, marvelling at what I was observing. Then suddenly, I realised I had to go to work.

I walked out the door knowing I had just experienced something very special. I was buzzing that day. I was solving problems with these wonderful creative haircuts, feeling absolutely on top of the world. Little did I know what was to come. I knew what I was experiencing wasn't dangerous. I knew whatever it was, was genuine. I knew something was opening up inside of me. I have never thought that this was drug-related. I had taken drugs on and off for the previous five years and never experienced anything like it. I know people who had taken a lot more drugs than I had, and this just did not happen to them, or anyone else I knew, for that matter.

I started to research seeing colours in a meditative state. I found out that it was common, that many people had experienced this phenomenon. I started to use more and more of my spare time to sit and meditate. I normally meditated for between five and twenty minutes at a time. I started to see more colours and more waves of light. Different shapes started to appear. It was almost like watching a TV being tuned. I wondered why I was experiencing this and how I had unlocked this new level of experience. I hadn't been a long-term meditator; I was just a normal guy experiencing amazing things. From what I've read online, these experiences come from lots of practice. I just felt full of gratitude. I felt like I had dedicated my life to experiencing new things. But this was on a whole different level. I didn't know this was possible. I was so happy.

The meditation meetings were going well. I started to lead the meditations, guiding people through a peaceful half an hour. When someone else led the sessions, I started to see more things. The circles and patterns of colours would suddenly whirl and swirl and crystallise and form actual images of things. Sometimes, I would see swirling water or birds flying in the sky or just something else equally as random. I knew these were visions of sorts. As my journey went on, my experiences and visions became more real and seemed to have more purpose and meaning. I believe the more random visions were my consciousness tapping into a larger energy field and picking things up.

Chapter 9

It happened on the last Thursday of the month in April 2016. My concept of what I believed was normal for my life changed irrevocably. This next stage of my story fills me with nervous exhilaration. To many, it's highly unbelievable, and bordering on insane. But I decided to break through the barrier of disbelief and share my story in its entirety… So here goes.

It was an extraordinary event that became central in what is now my extraordinary life. From that day forward, my life became mystical, energetic and supernatural. I was to experience things I'd never dreamt of, have encounters with beings from other worlds, have hundreds if not thousands of physically energetic phenomenal experiences, and, although I now don't think they're miracles per se, experience somewhat miraculous events. I'm still in awe of the whole thing. As of the time I am writing this, it is still happening to this day. This period of my life was the time I awoke to the true and complete nature of reality. The universe showed its hand to me, and I couldn't have been happier.

In this energetic, vibrational nature of existence, our universe merged with me and took me on an amazing adventure into another dimension. It wasn't in my sleep, but in the waking day, so I was under no illusion as to what I was experiencing. The timeline of events was just wonderful. It was everything I could have ever wanted it to have been. It was as if someone said to me, "Ed, you're waking up in this lifetime, how do you want it to go?"

On the day of the event, I was cutting a lady's hair. We got chatting and somehow got onto the theme of life and death. I asked her what she thought would happen to us when we die. She said, "We go to the astral planes."

I had never heard of this before, but I was interested. She went on to say how she believed us to be conscious, having a human experience and that when we died, our consciousness travels to another place, another dimension, and carries on existing there, and then perhaps, we re-enter the third dimension for another go at life, hopefully having learned from the previous life and receiving some kind of amnesia, so we don't remember past lives each time we re-enter.

I found her theory to be fascinating and not entirely unbelievable. I never thought too much about what happens after we die so I had no fixed opinion on the matter. She told me how she had left her body once, but got scared and snapped back in. She was happy for the experience, and it confirmed a big part of her belief system. She believed we merely use the body as a vessel to experience life here on Earth. I've come to realise so many religions and people believe this to be the case. For thousands of years, people have experienced this out-of-body phenomenon.

That night I went to bed early, about eight o'clock. As I lay in bed on my back, hands by my side, I had the intention of leaving my body. I shut my eyes and straight away it was as if I was being sucked into my bed, deeper and deeper, till the rest of the room felt very far away. I was quite shocked by this, but I went with it. I was fully awake, but I felt separated from The room, separated from the physical world I inhabited. What was even more remarkable was that my body started vibrating from head to toe, like I was plugged into something or like every cell had a mini generator attached to it and they were all switched on. I can't stress how physical this was, wearing, but at the same time, it felt extraordinary, different from an orgasm. It was from deep inside the whole body, but it had no single epicentre. It was a blissful vibration coming from everywhere. I was left in no doubt that I was experiencing something supernatural.

Suddenly, my feet, hands, chest and head started to heat up to, I reckon, 40–45 degrees. I mean, they got very hot very quickly. The body vibrations got quicker and more refined, and then all I could see were white lines zig-zagging across my eyes, even though they were still shut. The vibration went up another gear. I was nervous but very excited. The heat and vibrations were coupled with massive waves of bliss and ecstasy, far beyond any drug I'd taken. It's difficult to put into words the magnitude of this event. It's almost as though words could never do it justice. As all this was going on, the white lines I could see changed. I was now looking into three-dimensional blackness. Out of the blackness, I saw what looked like the shadow of a hill. From behind this hill, I saw a light, a little like the lights of a lighthouse rotating and peeking out from behind the structure.

To say I was exhilarated at this point is a massive understatement. I was holding on for dear life but happy about it. The lights then came from behind whatever was in front of me and came towards me, growing in size. It was a brilliant white light but not so bright that I couldn't look at it. As it came closer, my vibrations and the heat in various parts of my body became more intense, the feelings of bliss and ecstasy went to new heights, maybe even divine levels, I would say, if I wasn't there already. I felt like I was evaporating. I was no longer physical; I was consciousness undergoing an enormous event. I became aware of Nikki walking into the room. I heard and felt her getting into bed whilst all this was going on. I pulled myself out of it. It became too much to handle and I immediately regretted it. I rolled over onto my side and tried to get back to that place. The best I could muster was vibration and seeing the white lines, but I wasn't disappointed. I was in awe and felt so honoured to have experienced such an event.

When the experience was over, and I realised I couldn't

get back there, I lay in a foetal position wondering what the fuck had happened. My mind was triggered back to the previous miraculous events of a non-physical and physical nature in my life. I did a very quick dot-to-dot of experiences and realised that they were related and that it wasn't in my imagination.

Little did I know that this was some kind of activation. The next day when I woke up, I had never felt more alive in my entire life. I went to work feeling like a completely different person, the same but more awake, more vibrant. It's difficult to describe. It was like a drug but one that was full of love and peace and togetherness, and I felt dynamic, I could feel everything. I was seeing beautiful colours in the air, just floating around. My body was fizzing with life, actually fizzing, I could feel it all over, particularly in my hands, feet and head.

I walked into work and put out some fires straight away with confidence and a clear voice. I felt so good like my brain was sharper. I suddenly remembered that a new girl was starting that day. Her name was Zed. I was feeling so full of everything, and she could tell. I told her what had happened the night before right off the bat. She said, "Ed, you've woken up."

I said, "I'm not sure what you mean, but yes, I feel more awake to life than I ever have done."

There were times prior to this when I had felt incredibly in tune with everything. But this felt different. It was an unknown, new level of experience, and it was my conscious reality.

Zed only lasted a week in the salon as her work simply wasn't good enough. However, during that week, she put me in touch with Todd who was someone who was going to act as a stepping stone and show me that other people had experienced similar events. It turned out he was running a two-day workshop in a week's time on out-of-body experiences. I was stoked.

That night, after work, I googled reiki. My hands had had what felt like warm energy pouring out of them. When I placed them near each other, I could feel a force repelling each hand from the other. It felt like there was a ball of resistant energy between them. At times, it felt like they were glued together when I placed them near each other and moved them away slowly. I got connected to a guy named Arram Kong. He was a professional, very well-spoken oriental-looking man who spoke with such wisdom and insight. His website stated he was a reiki master and energetic healer. These were new concepts to me, but I was experiencing it, so I had to go with it. I told him my story, what had happened the night before and also a few things from the past. He said, "Ed, you've woken up. Im your first point of contact and I'm happy to help."

He went on to tell me that his understanding of the nature of reality is that it is energetic, and it works on vibrational frequencies, much like a radio. This reality we experience is Radio One, but there are many, many other stations. He presumed that what I had experienced was my people saying, "Hello." I burst into tears as I thought he meant Mimi, my grandmother, was speaking to me. He replied, "No, your other people, your helpers and guides."

I got off the phone amazed and shocked, but mainly humbled. It was probably the best phone call I've had or ever will.

I couldn't wait to get to bed. I wanted to experience it again. I got into bed and immediately the vibration started again but this time as my eyes closed it was as if another pair opened. It was like I was in a computer screen saver seeing tunnels and portals and lights coupled with feelings of vibrational bliss. I was travelling through an amazing multi-coloured portal; it was other-worldly. Suddenly I was viewing three beautiful purple pyramids in 3D, as if I was there standing in front of them. I was very conscious. I knew I was in my room but what I was seeing was the vista of another place. I then suddenly found myself viewing the moon or, at least, that's what I think it was. I was inside incredible geometric shapes, travelling through light and codes and symbols.

It was incredible. I felt superhuman. The amazing thing was that at no point did I feel scared or that I was having some kind of psychotic episode. It felt like the most natural thing in the world. Like it had always been there, waiting. Almost like 'I've done the time' and now I was being rewarded, or something.

I told Nikki what I was experiencing, trying my best to sound as sensible as possible. I didn't want to scare her. I didn't know where to begin or how. She took it well, I think. She seemed mildly concerned but was OK with it in general. She knew something was going on. But, hearing the reality of what was happening perhaps made her a little more prepared to believe me. I didn't blame her. How could anyone without experience of this believe me? But to be honest, I didn't care. I was having too much fun. It was beyond cool and so exciting.

That week was the week of miracles. On day three I woke up feeling superhuman. I think I felt like I was Jesus or something, which apparently is quite common when having an awakening. If not Jesus, I certainly felt like Neo in The Matrix, like I'd been unplugged from the reality which had gone before. I had a spring in my step and a glint in my eye and it wasn't going anywhere. I begged for this feeling not to go away. I felt so emotional. Tears would roll down my smiling face as I walked home or to the tube station or whenever I had a quiet moment to reflect. I was overflowing with elation and emotion. That night, I got onto the computer, Googling what I could about full-body vibrations, chakras, out-of-body experiences, and everything in between. It turned out there's a wealth of knowledge on these subjects. A whole world of words and concepts I had known nothing about. For me, I was encountering something brand new, but it was something that had already been well-researched and documented over the last 2000 years. And although I didn't need it, it validated my experiences.

On day four of my online quest for a deeper understanding of what was happening to me, I came across articles and books on 'awakening to your life's purpose' and other titles of a similar ilk. I was curious as throughout my life I always thought something big would happen but I had never thought it would be this; this was beyond my wildest dreams. Although the 12 steps of the Big Book did say I would have a life beyond my wildest dreams, I had thought that living without drink or drugs was as far as beyond my wildest dreams would take me.

I came across an article that asked me to open a book, any book, randomly pick a page and see where my finger was drawn to. Now, this may seem crazy, even to those that may have found it easier to believe my story so far, but I felt my hand track across the page like someone was doing it for me. My finger came down as if I was a puppet. The article asked me to do this on seven occasions on different pages. Each time I felt a guiding force moving my hand and finger across the page. I came down on the following words,

- My
- Your
- Vaccine
- There
- Help

Five was enough for me. It was such an astonishing experience to feel my hand being controlled by something else and, given that I was experiencing and seeing so much in the daytime, I didn't push my luck. This felt big enough. The article said that in the next day or two, something would happen that would be indicative of why this is happening and explain my path a little better. This was new to me. I had always gone through life relying on my intuition and mother nature to guide me; never had I relied on psychics or books

On day five I remember waking up and once again immediately thinking 'Wow, everything is so bright!'. I went for a walk in the park. Everything was glistening. It was amazing seeing everything shining brightly, like being on another planet yet still being here. I remember standing in a shop and a car drove by. I saw its reflection running slowly along the long strip lights in the shop. It was incredible to see. I was seeing light reflections that I couldn't see before. The sky was brighter and more luminous, as was everything else. It was a morning I'll never forget; it was as if I was experiencing heaven on Earth.

When I went back to the house, I gave Woody an enormous cuddle. It felt so special to be experiencing parenthood at this time, I told Nikki my eyesight was better, more enhanced. She told me I needed to calm down. It must have been difficult for her to see someone going through this and not fully understanding it. I kept most of my experiences from her at this point, not for any other reason than I still didn't quite know what was going on and didn't feel qualified to talk about it. I had to go and lie down for a couple of hours because my eyes were hurting. When I woke up, I walked outside and it was still the same, everything bright, luminous and sparkly. I was experiencing an absolute miracle. That night, the light show in my room from cars driving past and their lights reflecting in my bedroom was extraordinary. Nowadays, I'm not sure if I have just got used to it or it went away, but at the time it was exceptional. I had to phone Arram. I needed to speak to him.

My life had been turned upside down in such an unusual way. Everything had become supernatural overnight. He said he would give me an hour for free on Skype. I told him everything. He smiled at me and told me that there was a lot more to come. I was very excited by this. My life had become the best thing in the world, at least that's what I thought. He told me a little bit more about his views on reality. How everything is on a vibrational frequency and that even though we're able to create in this frequency, for example, make buildings, etc., nothing is really solid. This made total sense to me. He also told me I was an Indigo Child. I came here to wake up at this particular time to help in some particular way. Now, this really does sound out there but given what I had experienced over the last four days it felt right and the most sensible explanation. As he was speaking to me something astonishing happened. This again sounds completely crazy, but prisms of light flickered and moved on the computer screen around Arram's face. Suddenly, a non-human face popped through his skin like a hologram. I froze in wonder. I suddenly became aware of him asking me where I had gone. I said 'Nowhere', and we carried on talking. He told me I might see non-human beings every now and again and that I shouldn't be scared by this. I smiled to myself knowingly. I was elated at the prospect of seeing more epic stuff like that. I mean, who wouldn't be? He also said when the chakra system is activated as mine had been, our vision picks up more of the light spectrum., This is why seeing energy is possible.

When I got off the phone with Arram, I texted him and told him that he did something weird when we were speaking. He texted back, "I'm an alien if you know what I mean. Our souls or energy bodies can be non-human." I had just happened to see one in him. That's what he told me, anyway. I'm thinking to myself this is the coolest shit in the world but I must hold it together, so I'm not overawed by it. I found this surprisingly easy as the timeline of events was so beautiful and so perfect it was as if I had written it myself. Maybe I had. Maybe that's how it works. Perhaps we get to write our own awakening stories.

On day six, I experienced another miracle, but this time I had witnesses.

Nikki and I were sitting around the kitchen table having lunch with the kids. We spotted a huge fly on the window. I mean it was enormous, and the next thing I know, it was flying towards me. And I swear to you as it flew towards me, it's as though time slowed down and it froze in front of me, like in The Matrix when he has bullets flying towards him and they slow down. I stretched my hand out and plucked the fly from the air. I held my fist in front of me in amazement, knowing full well the fly was in there. I told Nikki that it was in my hand. "No," she said, "it's on the window." I opened up my hand and the fly dropped to the table, a little crumpled and seemingly dead. I reached out and touched it with my finger and it flew off. I mean this was fucking incredible or, at least, bizarre. But, given what had happened in the last five days, it seemed important. The kids loved it. I'm sure during that week, they were experiencing things as well. Woody was going crazy, but not in a bad way. It was as if he was experiencing the same energy I was, in some way.

My week of miracles passed, and it was time for Todd's course. It was amazing. It showed me how deep this stuff could go. He talked about his life and how he came to experience the paranormal from an early age. He seemed genuine and intelligent, so I trusted him. I was weary by this point but what he spoke of matched my experiences. He talked of the astral planes and energy and non-physical beings. He talked about how he and other people could leave their physical bodies.

Something amazing happened to me whilst in Todd's workshop. I was under an LED light meditation device which helps induce a meditative state of consciousness. I was lying down, eyes shut, enjoying the light show the LED lights provided, even with my eyes shut. I'm still not sure how it works, but it's a phenomenon called phosphene. Suddenly, my arms came out of my arms. It sounds crazy, but I was moving my energy arms whilst my physical arms remained on the floor. They felt heavy like they were stuck in mud but I definitely was in control of them. It was an extraordinary experience. The previous night, whilst at home on the sofa, I had been doing homework from the course. We were told to do energy work with the intention of something cool and energetic happening. I had, what in hindsight felt like, a prelude to the experience with my arms. The big finger on my right hand felt as if it was filled with helium and it floated up. I was moving it whilst looking at my physical finger not moving on the sofa. I'm sure doctors have got explanations for this but coupled with everything else I was experiencing, I was in no doubt that this was an energetic replica of my physical body.

In the coming weeks, I would often visit Highgate woods in the middle of the day and just lie there with my eyes closed and my energy arms would start floating. One day I thought I would keep my eyes open to see what was happening. It was incredible. I saw my physical arm floating a couple of inches above the grassy floor teeming and fizzing with energy. I could feel the energy all around my arm as it filled with helium and floated up. At this point, I thought I was about to levitate. I'm convinced levitation is possible after I had a few more experiences like this. It's very difficult to describe. People will always say this or that, but when the energy courses into my arm and I can feel rivers of it flowing through my fingers, then to experience lift off in one of my limbs is beyond explanation. It was just extremely special. On two or three occasions, my arms would rise and move and hold positions, which I could never hold by myself, for 45 minutes or more. This would happen whilst an extraordinary energy coursed in and around my arms and body.

I'd like to add, at this point, that I've had three EEGs in the last three years and all of them have come back showing I have a wonderful working brain with no signs of psychosis or anything that could create these things in my head. On the contrary, my brain wave patterns are in line with creativity, sharpness and awareness. Meditative science shows my patterns are in line with someone who experiences psychic phenomena.

My journeys to work became a phenomena in themselves. I would be driving, cycling, or on the bus with feelings of vibrational bliss streaming through my body and sometimes the energy would swirl around me and on top of my head. I only have drug references to go on when I talk about feelings of extreme bliss and ecstasy, but this was completely different to drugs. This was something way beyond what I knew was possible within the human experience; it was some kind of unseen energy passing through me and around me.

I started to see amazing cloud formations with colours in the sky. I experienced so much that tears would roll down my cheeks. By the end of this first week, I felt like I had been shown behind the curtain of our physical reality. At night I would vibrate in what felt like divine bliss. Every cell in my body was zinging and fizzing, I would see angels and other beautiful beings around me.

I would shut my eyes and I would see images of angels flying, either white angels with an orange background or purple angels with a black background These were not high-definition images, more like loose sketches, drawings with movement. Like snow angels in the snow flapping their wings.

I felt so honoured and privileged to be experiencing these things. It was very humbling as well, but mainly it was just so cool and exciting. I was like a child experiencing things for the first time and not being able to talk about them for fear of being ridiculed. I was just digesting everything.

I'd feel heat and see portals, spinning vortices of light with my eyes shut and I had a couple of occasions when I saw these things with my eyes open. I think I was able to see the portals with my eyes open because whatever frequency or dimension I was seeing was being imprinted onto my 3D reality. A little like looking into a room through a fish tank, I would experience both realities. I remember after a few months in, I woke up to go to the loo. I walked downstairs with my eyes half open. In the top half of my view was a mountain with the galaxy behind it, and in the bottom half was my house and whatever I was looking at to get to the loo.

One wonderful vision I had was of a luminous galaxy. I was lying in bed with my eyes shut one early evening. I was asking myself who or what was coming to me. It suddenly felt as if a page was turned and I saw a beautiful celestial event, clearer and brighter than any other visions I'd had. It was real-life photo quality but brighter and more luminous. I would go on to have many more experiences like this, like pages turning showing me a beautiful vista of some sort.

I was lying on the grass outside my shop. I was looking up at the sky and I saw this large, full-circle rainbow positioned horizontally, with the sun in the middle. It looked like a huge eye. In the days leading up to this, I had spent some time with my eyes shut in a meditative state, not for long, sometimes just a minute or two, and I would get visions of a big purple eye. Then this came to me, and I knew it was something very special, like God's eye looking at me, or something similar.

I went on to see more of these in the coming months. Eight I think, in total. I was experiencing energetic phenomena daily. I would wake up and my body would start vibrating. Like waking up in a lava lamp world, colours and geometric shapes were my staples in the mornings.

It was like I had a constant opening to another world just by shutting my eyes.

It's difficult to describe, but it's as if there is a body inside of your body, and it's switched on, vibrating and energising you using different rhythms at different times and in different parts of your body. Then, one area would get selected, and that area would increase in energy to the point where it permeated bliss and ecstasy. Then, I would see the portals and other geometric shapes, light patterns and visions of alien landscapes and views of galaxies in space. When I shut my eyes, in that blackness is where everything would happen. It would light up, and this could happen at any time I was awake, at work, throughout the day, in the morning or early evening.

Whenever I had a quiet moment, it would kick in. It's as if I was inside a computer program, inside an infinite space where things could appear and disappear and reappear again. They would come into view from the left or right or the top or down below. It was like a 360-degree arena that went behind me as well. This was when I eventually started to have encounters with what I believe to be non-physical helpers, angels and spirit guides.

Synchronicity

It was six weeks into this journey that I stopped going to the 12-step meetings. I found them difficult to sit through. My life had become what the meetings had promised, something completely beyond my wildest dreams. However, the environment involved a mix of people with poor mental health and others with big egos. Of course, there were some wonderfully wise heads there too. But I had a choice to make. I needed to decide whether to be in that environment or not. I knew that my time had come to move on.

I still remember my last meeting. I was buzzing with energy and just desperately needed to get away from everyone there. I just wanted to sit alone and process and enjoy what I was feeling. It wasn't them; it was me. I felt liberated walking out of that room. I was having the spiritual awakening of the century and there was no way I could stay in those meetings anymore. My time of introducing myself as, 'Hello, my name is Ed and I'm an addict' was over. The steps has been an incredible journey. I'd learned so much about myself and more. The lessons and learning I experienced would stay with me forever. I had learned how to reintegrate back into society. To give more than I take. To put others first as much as possible. And, most importantly, to take ownership of my shortcomings as a human being, to do everything possible to remedy this, to fight back against that over-extended sense of self that had ultimately sabotaged me and my relationships.

I was happy just to be alive. Completely satisfied with my lot.

I was on cloud nine, but this time it was not because I was coming off drugs. I was on cloud nine because I felt I was merging with the universe and the creative energies that created it and us. This is what it felt like to me.

To others, I may sound like a fantasist, but it was my reality. I was meeting aliens and angels and my chakras were opening. It took me by so much surprise and still does to this day. It was these experiences that compelled me to write my memoir.

People started coming into my life, mainly clients. I would get little windows of opportunity to share things, but never the big stuff. I had a really good reputation at my work and in general, and people just wouldn't understand if I started walking around saying I've met God and my chakras were opening, 'Oh, and by the way, we live in a three-dimensional matrix and there are more levels'. I didn't want to come across as arrogant and mad. I had to bide my time. I wanted to share my story in its entirety. I felt that my journey to this point in time was just as important as the reward I was experiencing. And besides, I was so happy just to experience it that I didn't feel the need to share it. I wanted to preserve the sacredness of the experiences. Words could not describe how at peace I felt and how excited I was, and still am to this day.

Nikki knew something was going on. She saw the experience of the fly at the table and the ripples of light go through the living room that night. It scared her a little, so I didn't want to expand on it with her too much, it's just how it was and what felt best at the time.

I'd been given this new skill, through a supernatural experience. I felt so honoured and privileged to be experiencing these things. It was very humbling as well, but mainly it was just so cool and exciting. I was like a child experiencing things for the first time, not being able to talk about it but just digesting it all.

In the late evening, mornings and lunchtimes became

the times of the day when I would experience things the most. Going to bed at night became such an adventure. I couldn't wait to see what was in store for me. I would lie down in bed and usually my feet and all my hands would start vibrating. Then the energy would move up through my legs, into my abdomen, neck, then head, and sometimes down my spine. Blissful vibrational ecstatic sensations would course through my body and I would have visuals. If my eyes were shut there would be a phenomenal light show followed by very quick experiences on what looked like alien landscapes, or I would have hexagonal shapes hurtling towards me spinning and gyrating.

This is going to be difficult to describe but I want to tell you about the first time I came across Buddha. It was after one of my sessions with Sky Acamesis, Todd's wife. Sky is a lovely person who helped me out for a few sessions in my early days where we did some energy work. I was feeling very much on top of the world and sharp. I was at Finchley Park Station when there was some kind of weather event in the sky. There was a black circle sort of floating behind or to the left of the sun. Just in front of the sun was the edge of a cloud, and further away from that cloud in the open sky was a square chunk of rainbow. As the sun hit the edge of the cloud, a face started to appear in high-definition. The face looked oriental at first, but then some kind of headgear started to appear. As the image crystallised, I was under no illusion. I was looking at Buddha. This surely was an extraordinary thing. I stayed rooted to the spot for minutes staring at this extraordinary event unable to move. I was frozen in amazement.

When I got home and over the next week I couldn't stop thinking about my encounter with what I know to be Buddha. So I bought a book on his story. It was a New York best-seller. The more I read about Buddha the more I realised that the similarities we shared were startling. We both came from a military family that lived in palatial surroundings. He may have been a prince of sorts. We both had our first spiritual experience at an early age, around eight or nine, and again in our late 20s, and then the big one when he sat under a tree aged 35 at the end of April. If you recall earlier in the book, I mentioned that it was the last Thursday in April when I was 35 that the big stuff started happening for me. There are many other details to our stories that are similar. I'm not saying I'm Budda, but there's a weird link there, which just made this journey for me even more special and obvious.

By this point, I was a couple of months in. I had let go of the fear that it was going to stop. I realised it was here and that the experiences would change, and that each phase would be different to the previous. I was feeling so good about everything. I was so eager for the next step and so willing to take on my mission whatever that may be. I had no idea what eventually would become, which is why I say ignorance can be bliss. Just knowing that something was coming was exciting enough for me.

Chapter 10

I find it hard to believe myself sometimes. It can sound so far-fetched to some people. I'm just an ordinary guy that just started to experience these phenomenal things and I want to share this.

I found myself going to meditation evenings as well as psyche training nights. I just knew I had to be somewhere where people understood this. I would walk into the room and other people around me would see I was having an awakening. My chakras were opening, my crown chakra had been opened enormously. The experience I had when this happened was mind-blowing. It often happened in my shop when I was alone, resting at the basins. Heat and energy and light exploding out of each energy centre, first my stomach, then my chest, then my heart, then my throat and then my head. It felt so supernatural, so divine. I just don't know how else to describe it. At a weekly energy/psychic course run by Kim Alexis, this lady came up to me and told me to read this book. It was a book that was channelled from a housewife in America. Her husband worked at NASA. They were a respectable 'normal' family. One day she started writing and it wasn't her. She wrote a book called We are the Arcturians. Writing through the wife, they described themselves as other dimensional beings that help on the planet in subtle ways, and that they were now able to have a more direct approach. They said it was something about the photon energy changing in our galaxy. Sounds ridiculous I know, but by this point, there wasn't much that surprised me.

I was a few chapters in when it happened. An extraordinary energy came and pierced the top of my head; however, it didn't hurt. The energy seeped through my body. It rendered me incapable of moving and in total bliss. It was completely beyond the feeling of an orgasm. Complete ecstasy moved throughout me. I've never injected heroin, but I can only imagine it to be something like this. Nikki came into the room and commented on how hot the room was. I said nothing. At this point, I was still unable to talk to her about it, which was a real shame, but I knew how it would sound. She would think I was losing my mind. In the following days, it was business as usual, wonderful vibrational divine experiences. I would shut my eyes and see colours in lights with feelings of overwhelming happiness and bliss.

I was researching on the Internet. I realised these things had been written about before, so that comforted me. I read articles about similar experiences happening to other people in slightly different circumstances.

I think it was on a Tuesday morning when I sat at the end of my bed, and I could hear my babies playing in the corridor. The kids and I had such an extraordinary time together. Having kids was a wonderfully spiritual experience for me. Having an energetic spiritual awakening at the same time was just beyond the realms of possibility in my mind. I felt like the luckiest person alive. I sat on the bed listening to them, fully dressed, ready for work. All I could see was bright orange. At the bottom of my view, I saw two luminous semicircles. It was stunning. They were bright and three-dimensional, like they were superimposed or something. It was like I was inside a TV set watching an object appear. They slowly started moving up into the centre of my view. I then realised what I was looking at; it was two enormous teardrop-shaped eyes within an oblong head. I freaked out in amazement and immediately opened my eyes. I knew I'd just had my first visual contact with an extra-terrestrial being. I can't stress enough how clearly this was happening right in front of me. It wasn't in my imagination or in the back of my mind. With my eyes closed, everything went orange and a three-dimensional being appeared right in front of me. I walked out of the house after giving my kids an enormous kiss and cuddle, smiling and practically skipping down the street. I felt so privileged. I knew they must exist. I've always had an open mind about living elsewhere, but had no idea how, when or if it would happen to me. Two weeks later, I sat on my bed again. The same orange appeared, and I could hear the same noises in the house. I saw those too luminous eyes, but this time they were coming in from a distance, straight towards me. I saw the being's head and upper torso, and that's when it happened. My head had some kind of orgasm. It was vibrating and tingling. It was like no other experience I had ever had. I believe it was the ET communicating with me. Whatever it was, it was lovely, and it was an amazing experience. I walked out the front door and the sun was shining. I held my face up to it with tears rolling down from my eyes. It was incredible. Deep down, I knew there was more to come. I knew that this was just the beginning, and it would've been irresponsible of them to pop up and leave. I took comfort in the fact that I knew this was an unfolding story. This had simply been an introduction and I couldn't be happier. I was ready for everything to come.

Weirdly, it made sense to me, why this could be happening to me. I had gone through stuff in life and not let it beat me or inflate me too much, and I was always looking to help. To help others and to make a big difference in life if I could. In the following weeks, I experienced pulsating, miraculous phenomena on nearly a daily basis. It became normal for me to experience this light, energy and vibrations return to my body at any given moment. I felt like I was being trained for something important, but I still had no idea what. It was a very exciting time. I never thought at any point that I was going insane. It was delivered in such a way that it made me feel very much at ease and was just so beautiful.

At night and in the mornings and sometimes during the day, I would see beings all around me. They were so wonderful and slender. They were loving entities and would send me blissful vibrations and feelings of support and love. I started to look up at the sky more. I had three experiences with UFOs in my back garden. Two were very far away, so they were disputable. However, one of them was about 200 metres from me. It was a horizontal disc-shaped craft. At this point, it seemed completely normal. Night times, between eight and eleven, were always so epic. I would lie there and just travel through portals, seeing beings all around me. It was as if I was travelling at the speed of light, seeing stars and planets whizz past me. I would sometimes see beings like schematic drawings. When my eyes were shut, I would be aware I was lying on my bed, but my view was through someone else's eyes, in another dimension perhaps. I would feel the beings touching my arms and legs. With each touch, a beautiful and inexplicable experience vibrated through my body. I felt like I was being upgraded and energetically trained to handle these experiences. Each time it would get stronger and stronger till I couldn't take any more. It was straddling the borders of pleasure and pain.

In the following days, I felt like I was levitating. I was so incredibly immersed in what I was experiencing, whilst at the same time separated from my physical body. There was this one day, I was walking to my car to get something when I decide to sit on the side of the road on a log and meditate. A white van drove by, and the guy looked at me and shouted something unpleasant. I ignored it, I could barely even make out what was said. I was in a state of complete bliss. It was then that I had an instant out-of-body experience. I saw hands being placed on my head. When I got up, I was walking up Wood Lane in Highgate. My vision was blurred. When it finally cleared, everything looked the same. What I mean by this is that I couldn't see or recognise the difference between the rows of houses, the cars, the people... Everything lost its meaning. I had no idea what was happening. All I knew was that I was existing. A consciousness was looking through my eyes without really recognising one thing from the next; it was just one big thing. I looked at my hands and I didn't recognise them. I knew they belonged to me and that I could operate them. But that was it, I had no attachment to them. It felt as bizarre as it sounds.

After ten minutes I started to wonder how I could continue in that state. I couldn't possibly carry on with my day or talk to anyone like that. Could I? I walked into the bank in Highgate and did what I had to do robotically and seamlessly. When I went back to work, it started to drift away. I could feel my sense of self returning. Although I felt extremely privileged to experience that 45 minutes of complete removal, I was happy I was coming back. It was such an enlightening experience. I researched it online and learned that this stage was something that people had encountered on their awakening journey.

That same year, 2016, in September, I flew to Morocco with my brothers Harry and Max for a week's surfing. We had been looking forward to this trip. From the moment we got there, we fell completely into the flow of things. Everything just seemed to work out the way we planned it. We got the waves we wanted, we met lovely people and all the logistics just worked, which is tough in Morocco. We were there when a lunar event occurred, I can't remember which one, but it was one that doesn't come around very often. I was woken by a dog barking at 4 am. I got up, went to the loo, came back and just lay down on my bed. Suddenly, a light went off in my room. It was as if someone had lit a flash bomb. I was pinned to the bed with extraordinary, ecstatic, blissful energy. My hand was taking the brunt of it. It was half cupped, with my thumb and forefinger shaped a little like the scarab beetle. I was unable to move. I just stayed put and relaxed. This was a new kind of energy. It was nothing like I had experienced before. So much stronger and localised. and the electricity, vibrations and blissful feelings were so great. When it stopped, I jumped up and woke my brothers up. I told them what had happened, and they got back into bed and just smiled.

The next day, I was lying in bed in the early evening, and I had a vision. When I say vision, it could have been an astral projection moment. Either way, my whole reality changed with a pop. I found myself staring at a pair of spectacles in space. They were glistening under a silver light, and rotating, as if to show me the beauty of the glasses.

It all came to a head on that third day. It was early morning, and I felt an intense energy coursing through me as if a million volts were being pumped into my chest cavity with every beat of that metronomic knocking sound. My vision was going all over the place. Although so much was going on, I was acutely aware of the white noise that seemed to fill my space. Suddenly, everything calmed, just enough for me to be conscious of where I was. I found myself in this multi-coloured room. The colours were moving in a psychedelic fashion. As my sight came more into focus, I realised something was standing in front of me. As it slowly turned around, it revealed its big head and large deep-set, teardrop-shaped eyes. It was wearing a wonderful outfit. It was beautiful. It spoke to me. I could hear the words, but not from where it was standing. I could hear them in my head. It was communicating with me telepathically. There was no mistaking it. It wasn't voices in my head, it was more like a microphone was there and it was using it to speak to me. It was clear, concise and reassuring. Not once did I feel that this was a negative experience.

I looked over at the clock when it finished. It was 5 am. The whole thing had lasted about an hour. I got up and walked to the balcony. As I looked out to sea over Anchor Point, I could see these ghost-like shapes that resembled jellyfish floating across the water. I think I was seeing some kind of craft in between the dimensions.

I felt myself disappear into the beauty of it all. I stood there, coming to terms with what had just happened to me. I was so happy, grateful and humble.

I realise now that what I've said goes far beyond the realms of what most people find credible. I can almost see many of you putting the book down at this point. I'm cool with that; however, should your curiosity take you through the rest of this book to see how it ends, you won't be disappointed.

After Morocco, things ramped up. The energy was coming in all the time, and I was having more contact with the beings. I say contact, but it wasn't always communication in the way we understand communication to be. I remember one experience; I got the urge to lie on my bed. It was about 7 pm, maybe a bit later. As I lay there, my feet began to crackle and fizz, like water was being trickled on them, I would also feel tapping like someone was knocking at the door, on the soles of each foot. That's when it started. I was in a state of complete and utter bliss. I could feel the vibration coming up through me from my feet to my legs, then chest and finally to my head.

It filled every part of me with an unimaginable sense of euphoria that I can't even put into words. As soon as the vibrations hit my head, all vision ceased, as well as feeling for the outside world. I was completely engulfed in light. Lights were flashing around me, and three-dimensional shapes danced before my eyes until they eventually transformed into swirling hexagram flowers or pyramids. Then I saw that beings were being drawn. They were unfinished but still able to move. It felt as if I was there, but I was still also aware that I was still lying on my bed. The beings lightly touched my legs and arms.

At times, the touch felt like a pinprick, which caused an extraordinary energetic event throughout my body that would touch me at a divine level and beyond. This sort of experience became the norm. When the energy came through my head, it felt like a sublimely ethereal honey-like substance being poured slowly over my brain.

One night I was part of some extraordinary ceremony, another night I would see machinery and what looked like a spacecraft. On one occasion, I was inside what seemed like a spacecraft. It felt like home. I felt so relaxed, which made me open my eyes and I realised I was in my bedroom. I tried quickly to get back to where I had been. What resulted was a vision of being inside the spacecraft with the reality of my bedroom imprinted over the top, like when you look through a fish tank into a room and you see both views on top of each other. It was fucking unbelievable.

I had this heart energy centre activation once. It was like something straight out of a science fiction film. I was sitting at the end of my bed on my chest, at about 8:45 in the morning, fully dressed. The kids were playing in the hallway. I just shut my eyes and said a prayer for the day.

Suddenly, I was up in this huge tree with this big blue being like Dr Manhattan in The Watchman. He was ripped. Then I was in his house, which contained all sorts of amazing objects and shapes. The house looked as though it was made out of wood. Then I found myself in some sort of classroom with little blue beings. Then, as quickly as I had been transported there, I blinked, and I was in a garden where this amazing tree grew out of the ground. It was multi-coloured like a rainbow. It proceeded to open up my chest area and the next thing I knew I was back, lying on my chest at the end of my bed with my heart chakra going bananas, vibrating and emanating extraordinary energy. It was a beautiful experience. I felt very emotional afterwards and was relieved that I had had it, to be honest. At this point, I had had so many other chakra activities but not heart ones, so I felt very special on many different levels.

In the next few months, I had experiences with religious deities and other inter-dimensional beings, all whilst having extraordinary crown chakra activations. There were more experiences inside spaceships, albeit very quick ones, and I enjoyed conversations with God. It felt beyond real. But it was real. Everything that had been shown to me and everything I had experienced had been as clear as day, so there was never any doubt in my mind.

I went through many, many experiences during those next few months: hundreds. If time permitted, I would have loved to have included each and every one of them here. However, my aim isn't to list every experience I've had. I want to share the process I went through to get to the stage I am now. After 18 months of various experiences, they changed gear. My experiences now had what felt like a more important purpose. It's all very well having these wonderful experiences, but if no one's benefiting from them other than myself, what was the point? Strangely, I feel like I've been inspiring people and giving warmth to people my whole life, whether friends or strangers in need, family members in trouble or the thousands of clients I've met and chatted to over the years. I've always enjoyed listening and talking. But now my message and vibe have an extra layer, an extra dimension.

By this stage, I had been attending a meditation meeting

for a few months. It was held in a beautiful townhouse in Kensington, which belonged to a lady called Carol. The top floor was stunningly decorated with bright colours, art deco pieces and ancient Chinese statues. She channelled very high energy and had had amazing results with healing.

She became a really good friend and still is to this day. Carol was such a character; every time I saw her she had just bought another house or flat in one of the energetic hotspots in the West Country. The energies that I experienced in her group meditations were so amazing. They felt almost miraculous. In the centre of her living room, she had these enormous crystals. It was a beautiful, Georgian-style living room with huge windows. After about six months, I wanted to move in a different direction, and I found that being in a group environment wasn't working as well as it had been.

If I had had any doubts over the authenticity of my experiences with meeting what I now know to be spirit guides, they would have been laid to rest as such meetings now happened so often. Whenever I was in a deep state of relaxation, my body would start vibrating energy. It felt like something between my eyes and around my forehead would turn on this mini generator that made me feel energised. The feeling is indescribable, thoughts being channelled at an intense level, coming from parts of my brain and beyond. It was a whole new way of existing in the moment. Electricity and light, feelings of God and angels.

My eyes would close then I would suddenly be in front of some kind of person or being not from this world. For instance, I once met with one that had a cat/fox-type head and face. It was dressed in this cool-looking tight space suit. She told me she was from the Galactic Council. My eyes were not always closed during these experiences, however, which again confirmed the genuineness of what was happening. I once met with this Chinese-looking guy who put his hands on my shoulders. I then proceeded to vibrate in divine bliss for about 15 minutes with my eyes open lying on my bed at 8 pm.

The intensity of pleasure I felt when entering different dimensions went beyond anything I could put into words. to explain. I never knew why any of these things were happening to me. The amalgamation with the world and beyond was without comparison to anything I knew possible in this world. I would think something and then it would happen. For instance, I might be thinking of an old friend who I hadn't spoken to in ages, and the next thing you know, they would call me, or their name would randomly pop up out of nowhere after not having seen them for months or years.

Things just kept working out so well at work; it was as if everything had been scripted ahead of time! Certain people would walk by me at the right time. Yes, the sceptics will call these coincidences, but they were happening so regularly that even my best friend Jordan, who is a sceptic, was starting to see something was happening to me.

I started to have more visions of Buddha. I also had three experiences with Jesus. The weight of what I am saying doesn't escape me. His name comes with a lot of gravity. I'm not a Christian per se. I also know at this point, if you didn't think I was mad before then you may start to think it now. But these weren't dreams. They would sometimes occur when I was awake in the middle of the day. The energy enters me, and I would have visions of spiritual leaders and deities. I had to take notice. I have to take it as real and give it the respect it deserves. What else could I do? I couldn't just ignore it. One thing I was certain of was these religious leaders existed. They were extraordinary. I believe there were most probably non-human, multi-dimensional incarnations, to help people with their human experiences. I don't subscribe to any religion. My experience has been one of oneness. That all these beings are fighting for the same cause, they just have their own stance and look around for energy. It was humans who separated them and compartmentalised them and attached different dogmas around each of them. I experienced deities from Christianity, Hinduism and Buddhism. So, I can't be all of these religions at once. So, I figure they're all one and the same thing. Just marketed differently.

I stopped wondering why I was experiencing this. Why me? I had been through so much shit in my life and overcome so many things. I'd had astounding challenges which nearly took my life, and had extremely wonderful experiences and enjoyed great privileges, all wrapped into one; I had seen the extremes of both the good and the bad in life. But I'd always prospered. I always climbed onto what was right, even in my darkest hour. I never gave up. I fought fire with fire. When I had speech problems, I became an actor. When I felt hatred for my dad, I turned it into an abundance of love for him. When I struggled to find the motivation to get off the couch, I ran a marathon. When I felt alone, I surrounded myself with people. And when I couldn't bear myself, I decided to help others.

I was on some kind of path that I knew nothing about. Although I maybe wasn't fully prepared, I was willing, and I fully committed myself to it. I would openly affirm to the sky, do as you will, I trust you, I love you and I want to help. I wanted to take my help to the next level. I wanted to move beyond helping my kids, helping drug addicts, helping people at work, helping someone with their shopping or crossing the road, or whatever it may be. I wanted to help on a whole new level. I knew my story alone could help people, and I'm sure that this will be more relevant as time goes on. But I was beginning to get a sense of a new kind of energetic help, a supernatural help, I could offer. The sort of help that I didn't know existed other than in science fiction stories. When the energy centres in my hands started up, it was so palpable, like I was holding big hot footballs, feeling the universal energies coursing through my arms into my body. I knew this energy had to be put somewhere, but I had no fucking idea what was to come next.

On the evening of May 27, 2017, everything became much clearer. Nikki was in Germany working, the kids were asleep, and I was lying in bed. It was about ten o'clock at night. The energy started coming into me. At this stage, it had happened so many times before, I thought I was prepared for it. This time, however, was very different. It felt stronger. It was getting faster, building up in my chest cavity, in my head, in my legs, and in my arms. It was all over me. My eyes shut down, my crown chakra opened up and I was seeing the lights and colours and portals on a whole new level of intensity. This was a truly magnificent experience. I remember thinking, *'Holy shit! I really have left Kansas now!'* Suddenly, my back arched, and everything calmed down. Amongst all the energetic goings on, I felt something beautiful take over my body and my mind. I started speaking and it wasn't me, I tried to interject, just to check I was able to, and I wasn't. I was observing and experiencing this, as if there was a piece of glass in front of me, preventing me from coming through, I didn't mind though. It was beyond wonderful. Suddenly I heard my voice speak out into the room, "Hello, my name is Helioah. We are the Arcturians. We are sending you and your planet this dimension of light. Please accept this transmission."

I was then incapacitated on the bed for 15 minutes. Energy was streaking through my body, sending me into divine bliss. It was almost too much. I then realised this so-called fifth dimension of life is what I had been receiving for the past 15 months. It had to be. It finally all made sense. This invisible light, the sensations I felt, and the way it was being delivered to me all made perfect sense.

I don't want to intellectualise the experience. All I know is that this is how it went down and how it has continued to this day. I woke up the next morning at about 7:30 when it started again. The energy poured into me but this time there was no voice, I just saw a clear image of a being with a big head and big eyes moving around in front of me. The energies and sensations I experienced were beyond words. It was perfect. they were letting me know that it wasn't a dream and that it was really happening. I got onto my knees by the side of my bed, still vibrating. Feeling blessed, I put my hands together, and I said, 'Thank you', and that I accepted that this was how God, or whatever word you want to use, was going to work through me and that I couldn't be happier.

When I Googled 'trance mediums', the first site that came up was an experienced woman named Donna Stuart. She had done stage shows where she would give people wonderful information about themselves and had earned her reputation as being 'the real deal'. Based on these reviews, it seemed like a great place to start looking for help in finding out more details regarding my situation with mediumship. She was a family woman who seemed genuinely friendly and caring; I got a great vibe from her! I told her my story over Skype, and I was keen to ask her for her help. I remember our first session. I booked a local treatment room, but there were Internet connection issues. I remember as soon as we were on Skype together my whole body started vibrating – and then the connection went. It was, however, an exciting experience and I had to come back for more. During the next session, there were no Internet issues. Whatever was trying to channel through me had been waiting for this moment. I could feel it coming, but it was as if the universe wanted me to live in anticipation of what was happening to me. I felt waves of bliss coming through me and experienced an energy that made everything else seem so trivial. I felt like I was giving birth through my body into my mouth and out the top of my head. Donna said she could see the energies that wanted to come through. She described a vision of an old man with white hair holding a staff. She described the character I'd had an experience with all those years ago to a T. I believe that the energy took on this form as a way of presenting itself. I think it's just some kind of extraordinary energy put into picture form for the receiver. At the end of the session, Donna looked at me and told me I had done very well. Overcome with emotion, I burst into tears.

Later that day, I walked into my house, which was bustling with movement. The kids were running around. I could tell they had just eaten dinner. They ran up to me and I hugged them tightly as though I hadn't seen them in years, even though it had only been a few hours.

"Daddy!" they shouted happily.

I stayed at eye level, staring at them for a few seconds, then said, "Something special is happening to daddy, and I couldn't be happier."

By this point, I was feeling like the perfect candidate for this. I'd accepted it was happening.

I don't have any religious or spiritual beliefs, yet I live a life that demonstrates these principles most of the time. When things happen to people around me, whether it be my friends or strangers, I'm deeply affected by them and do what's in my power to help. Owning a hair salon means being constantly around people who trust you and want to tell you everything. If I could deliver the messages and guidance that was being sent through me in a sensible, plausible, educated and grounded way, I felt like I could change the world, or certainly my clients in Highgate, anyway.

I was sitting in the bathroom of my salon, which I had found to be the cheapest and most private place to hold the sessions. I'd had about four or five sessions with Donna at this point. She had been coaching me on receiving the energies with more intention and concentration as opposed to just letting them take me whenever they felt like it. This, in turn, meant I started to have fewer experiences. I was fine with this. I had had my fair share over the last two years, and now I felt these experiences had more direction. It was around then that something changed during one of our sessions. My consciousness went elsewhere, as if part of my brain switched off for a moment, as high-definition clarity came out of nowhere. Words flowed freely from my lips into the air, "He's doing very well."

I immediately burst into tears; it was an overwhelming experience. It was the first time I had intentionally spoken in an altered state. Donna was great. Through her experience, she knew just how to handle me and the energy that was coming through. As our session progressed, more words followed. It was very difficult for me to allow them to speak through me, to surrender myself to encounter. It was unnerving at times, although I did feel very special. Donna could see I was the real deal, and she trusted the energy coming through me. However, my process of channelling perplexed her. Usually, a trance medium will go into the sleep state where they're not conscious of what's happening. I was always fully conscious. It was impossible not to be alert with all those energies and fantastical energised experiences entering and exiting my body. There was no way I was going to fall into a sleep state. To merge with them, it was like I just had to relax whilst, at the same time, have thousands of volts going through my body. Or that's what it felt like. People have said that at times I started chanting 'Om'. Although I am fully conscious, if the connection is very strong it evaporates from my head, like waking up trying to remember a dream. But I had to take my time, I had to learn to control these energies. I had progressed in that I was able to call on them at times, but I had to learn to control the bucking bronco reaction caused by the intense electricity when they entered me. But this was what Donna was for. She was there to help, and she did so, immensely. After ten weeks of weekly sessions, I had six energies coming through me, all of them beautiful high energies that surrounded me with golden white light whenever they came in. I was learning to anchor that energy. Each had its own voice. Some sounded a little female, others were powerful, and others were just other-worldly. My voice box and throat energy centre would open up and get worked during these sessions. I could feel my voice box and throat and trachea changing and flexing. The energies would speak of great work to do. They would tell me they were from other worlds and other dimensions of existence. They said they were here to help activate and heal people on a new Earth. At the time, I wasn't sure what this meant; however, in hindsight, I now know they were referring to the pandemic. No matter what our stance is on what is happening right now, one thing we all have to admit is that life has changed forever, and the Earth seems very different. So, for me, the pandemic was like another perfect synchronisation in my story.

Whilst learning to perfect my channelling abilities, I was a little concerned about how people would take it. If they didn't think I was mad before, this would convince them. I kept what was happening to myself. It felt like the right thing to do at the time. I've had great intuition my whole life and I felt like it was all geared towards this moment of trust. This happened to me at a point in my life when I hadn't had a drink or drug in three years. I was physically very fit and emotionally stable. I had this confidence that I can't describe. I could be in a room with anyone, from any walk of life, and remain non-judgemental, unafraid, and able to help and lead when necessary. However, I didn't want my experiences to be impacted by other people's doubts or opinions. I wanted to wait until I had established full control. I found that the divine energetic encounters with beings had started to creep in again more regularly in the first three months of my sessions with Donna. Although, I did feel that the beings were quite aloof. I didn't always know in which order they were coming, and they didn't say where they were from exactly. And I certainly wasn't getting any names. I wasn't bothered by this, however. In fact, I was almost happy about it. I'd experienced so much that these facts, names and places were unimportant to me. If they were to suddenly say, 'Hello, we are this or that or from here or there', I feel, in retrospect, it would have been too much to handle. It would've unbalanced me. I might have lost my identity and taken on theirs. I may have started walking around saying the Arcturians are here, or Captain Alien is now working through me and I'm not important. I was happy to take it slowly. After all, this was still unbelievable to me. I was still in awe and very much still a passenger in this experience.

Another type of regular experience I had was with UFOs. There is one specific experience I want to share. For me, it dissolved any doubt anyone may have had regarding what I was going through. It wasn't a hallucination; I'm not going mad (I don't think) and I'm not a liar. So for me, it was as real as the book or device you are holding to read this. It was winter in 2018, and Hakile and I were working in the shop. It was a rainy evening, at about 6 pm. Hakile was washing a client's hair and I was on the phone to my potential landlord, trying to negotiate rent for new premises six shops down from mine. I was having a tough call with him; he was a typical landlord, solely money motivated. The reason I was considering moving shop was quite unusual. Two months prior to this, I had been to see Kim Alexis, the lady who ran the weekly energy/psychic course I mentioned earlier on in the book. She told me I was going to have a new shop by the end of the year. At first, I didn't believe her. The two months passed, and I wasn't even looking for a new business and the year was nearly up. Then, lo and behold, the owner of the barbershop six doors down from me walks in and asks if I wanted to buy his business. So, I'm on the phone to the potential landlord, and as I'm getting frustrated on the phone, I look over the road at the park. I then move my eyes to look about 20–30m above the park, and I see a light glowing. It was as clear as the brightest star in the night sky. I stared at it for a couple of seconds, then the light expanded to about three or four metres in length and then shot off at warp speed. I was stunned. It had happened, I thought to myself. I had just seen a spaceship move away and vanish into thin air leaving a trace of light behind it. And this had happened in my physical 3D world. In all honesty, I can't remember ending the call. I called out to Hakile.

"I've just seen a craft of sorts, hovering then moving off at lightspeed, or warp speed," I said.

It felt like such a privilege. Now, any normal person would have taken Kim's word as gospel. This was a sign that I should take the shop. Not only had Kim predicted it, but one of my galactic brothers or sisters had turned up to the phone call and given me one of the best experiences in my life. But me being me, I didn't take it. Something got in the way, and I convinced myself that the UFO sighting was offering me a choice because I had doubts about the business deal, and I felt as though I should stick to my galactic stuff. Looking back on it, I always regretted that decision, which is unlike me as I don't think I have regretted anything else in my life. But there were too many unknowns with the landlord and I was in a lot of personal debt. So that was that.

My sessions with Donna continued. We held them in the toilet in my salon until I finally bought shutters for the windows. By this point, I felt like I was living two lives. I had my family, work and social life, and then I had these extraordinary supernatural experiences that were happening to me on a regular basis. Was I some kind of Shaman, medium or channel? I just didn't know. I didn't care. What I was experiencing was beyond what I thought was possible and it gave me such love and warmth. It was also making me a better person in ways I didn't know possible. For instance, my stammer had all but disappeared, I felt I was able to decipher problems more quickly, I felt more empathy towards people, and I also felt an inner confidence and strength, which was there before but was now enhanced. My relationship with my kids, my understanding of them and our bond was so big, so special. We would often shed tears of joy over the silliest things. We would have wonderful spiritual conversations. I would feel the energies in and around them when I was with them. They would start to say things like, "Daddy, in my dreams tonight I'm going to visit other dimensions, other planets, I'm going to meet angels and friendly aliens."

These times were priceless. I look back on them and just think 'Wow!'. My son Woody's artwork is exceptional. He has a bit of genius within him. My daughter Agatha is the most beautiful, kind-hearted, and giving person I know. I'm not saying my son isn't these things, but my daughter exudes it in a way you don't see very often.

I was happy living my two separate lives. I hoped that one day the two would merge, but I was and still am nervous about this prospect. Sometimes a client would sit in my chair and during our conversation, if I got the feeling or they said something, we would talk about the nature of reality, and I would share some of my experiences. That was always welcome, and it certainly gave the client a little bit more than a haircut. But I was, and am still, scared that people will think I'm crackers. So, with this in mind, I felt I needed some medical evidence. I knew for sure what was happening to me, and I also knew that something would show up in some kind of brain scan. How could it not? I can invoke such physical electrical experiences on demand, that there had to be some kind of physical effect on my brain. I went about researching how to get an EEG. I got in contact with a company called Brain Train UK. I told the director, Stuart Black, my story and he was eager to come and scan me for free. This was great as it would usually have cost over a thousand pounds. He said he'd scanned the creative force behind Buffy the Vampire Slayer's brain as he is known as a creative genius. He was aiming to map the brains of people with different skill sets. So, he was keen to map the so-called medium channelling brain. He came to my shop and wired me up to his machine. He put a skull cap on me that made me look like a Russian cosmonaut. As soon as he switched on the machine while I was under normal consciousness, he let out an expression of surprise and said, "Wow, your alpha frequency is huge!"

At that time, I had no idea what this meant. I've come to know now that this is referring to the subconscious or the meditative frequency. It transpires that in awake states I have access to my subconscious. We did a session, and I went into the altered states, and when I finished, Brian looked shocked but happy. He said he needed to go away and have a look at the results and would get back to me. He called me a week later and told me, "I've not seen that happen to anyone nor have I seen a brain map like it."

He said there were no flags of psychosis, and that I had an exceptional working brain with the addition of being able to access and control my brain frequencies at will; especially my alpha and gamma frequencies and, on occasion, my theta range. This really excited me. I had an official document saying I wasn't mad. I would happily stand up in a court of law, and say 'Look. This is what happens to me'.

My sessions with Donna were going so well. She would invite other people into the meeting via Skype. The energies would come through me, and they would address whoever was sitting in front of me. They wouldn't give specific information like dates and names, but they would certainly give relevant information to that person on where they were in their life, and that resonated as true for them. The energy coming through me would say, "We renew time on Earth now. The veils of reality are thinner and more can be accessed."

They would talk about everything being a vibrational energy frequency and that three-dimensional life is like a dense energy hologram; it's here for us to experience, to learn from and grow. They would talk about other levels of existence. They said they were here to help enlighten people about this fact and to work on people's energy bodies. The energy body and the mind are a little bit like the ghost body or the light body that operates alongside the physical body. I thought it was time that I started to offer my experience to other people and to grow as a channel. Soon enough, I had three to five people coming every other week to my salon. The energy would come in. I would sweat with nerves, but I would finally manage to let go. This is still something I'm working on. What people saw astounded them. My face would change, my voice would change, and they would know that Ed has left the building. The energies would stream through me. I mean, it was off-the-charts bonkers. But when I came out of it, everyone in the room would just be in awe of the experience. They said they had felt the healing and energetic phenomena moving throughout their bodies. I couldn't be happier. I would sometimes cry when I came out of it. I was so happy to help people in this way.

Never in my wildest dreams did I think this could happen to me. But when I looked back at the various encounters I had with spaceships and other-worldly beings, and considered the energy that would course through my body, even whilst I was awake, it made sense to me that this was my calling. I firmly believe that anyone who has had these experiences can help people in the same way I did. Despite this realisation, I needed to know more. I wanted to meet more people that knew about this type of thing; after all, I didn't move in spiritual circles. I was just a regular guy to whom this was happening. OK, when I say regular, I've always considered myself slightly above average, truth be known. I've had lots of experiences in life, but I am still a normal person. I had never read about any of this stuff, and I had no idea it was out there. So for me, I felt very much part of the unknown. I started to get in touch with people that I knew. I heard about a college called the Arthur Findlay College of Psychic Science. This was a mecca for mediums and channels and all things strange. So I went there for a two-day course. It was held in this wonderful old building that looked like my boarding school, Salisbury Cathedral School. When I arrived, I felt slightly out of place. There were lots of new-age-type people there. I was one the youngest and I felt like my background was different to everyone else around me. The educators, who were the world's best mediums, immediately singled me out as someone with talent. But typically, as I had experienced at school with my sports teachers, they were extra hard on me. I didn't mind this at school, but mediumship and channelling were new to me. I needed to feel held. The whole establishment seemed very old-fashioned to me. The way they experienced trance mediumship was very different from how I experienced it.

My consciousness flies up and out the top of my head, whereas the way they taught and expected it to be was to go inwards into a normal sleep state. Anyway, I was pleased I went, but I couldn't wait to leave. I'd almost gone there to do what I had to do; just by being there I was admitting to myself that this was happening, and this was starting a journey for me.

When I got back into my sessions with Donna, she told me she knew I would struggle there, but she was also glad I had gone. It was important for me to get a picture of the industry, so to speak.

My next stop was Holland. One of the educators at the college inspired me. In fact, she was the only one in the college to inspire me. Her name was Nicole Haas. She realised that my consciousness went up and out. Where she worked in Holland, they did EEG scans, but they followed Max Cade's programme of Mind Mirror Mapping. Max Cade was a government nuclear physicist who was also interested in the brainwave patterns of anyone who experienced a different version of life, such as psychics and Swami gurus. He also mapped creative and industry leaders, just to see what happens to their brainwaves in certain situations. After years of research, he put together an assortment of brainwave patterns that occur when certain states of consciousness are experienced. He coined the term *the awakened mind pattern*. This pattern occurs when a sweet spot occurs in the brain. It is when we have access to our subconscious and all the connections through the different brainwave patterns are equal, that real creativity can happen, he said. He also found out that spiritual leaders have these patterns occurring regularly. I couldn't wait to get under the machine. When the session was finished, the lady conducting the test looked like she had done this before. I told her I'd had one clinical EEG but never with the Mind Mirror Map.

She showed me my brainwave patterns, normal consciousness and the altered state. It showed I had an awakened mind pattern going on. The other brainwave patterns suggested I was connecting to another field of consciousness. This was so exciting for me. It was another body of evidence that helped cement me on my new path. I was excited to show people if I were ever to be questioned about my experiences and channelling. I wanted to say, 'Look here, check this out'. It felt like I was a kid walking into a sweet shop for the first time.

When I got back to the UK, my sessions were getting better and better. People who had started to feel certain ailments in their bodies were healed after the sessions. Unfortunately, my marriage with Nikki wasn't going as well as my sessions were. It was deteriorating fast. Something had to give. We had tried counselling, but not only did it not work it created a bigger divide between us. I knew this relationship wasn't right. But how could I end it? We were both so close to our beautiful kids. I can't put into words how special morning cuddles were and playing with them during the day. My memories of teaching them how to walk started to become painful. I couldn't bear to think what experiences we could miss with the family not being together. These extraordinary mirror images of the two of us absorbed everything we gave them. Everyone could see how loving these kids were. If Nikki and I had done anything right, it was these two kids. They lit up every room and still do. Woody's art was just getting so good. His pictures were extraordinary, and we kept every single one, framed and mounted. Agatha was just such a beautiful daughter. She just couldn't do anything wrong in my eyes. I absolutely loved her to bits. She was such a very good girl who was always up for anything. Could we do this to them? There was no other option. Nikki and I were starting to argue more and more in front of them. I knew I had to make a call, but I just didn't want to. How could I break up this family? How could I put them through exactly what had happened to me? It was just history repeating itself. How pathetically predictable. But I knew I had to do it. Our marriage had started on this journey to its end a couple of years earlier. But a move like this takes time. There's an assimilation process that has to take place before the day of reckoning arrives. After the last ever argument, I sat on the kitchen floor crying. I just knew it was time. I looked into my son's eyes and said, "Woody, I'm going to go and sleep in a different building, but I'm going to be here every morning and evening. You'll never know I'm not here."

The tears flowed down my face as I spoke, just as they are doing now as I write this. He looked at me, and said, "Daddy, I don't want you to go."

His little face looked sombre. I held him so tightly. I told him that I loved them both very much and that they would always be in my heart. This extraordinary boy looked at me and said, "It's okay, daddy, you'll be so quick I know, I won't even know you're not here, and you're always in my heart so it's OK."

He was four years old and my daughter was two. I felt she was a little too young to understand, but she soon did.

I lived in a shared flat just around the corner from the family home. It was a very painful six months. I suddenly found out what separation anxiety was. I cried myself to sleep many times. I woke up at five o'clock every morning with a broken heart and I'd start getting ready to go to the house to be with my babies. I arrived by seven so that they would never see that I wasn't there for them. Sometimes, they would find me asleep on the sofa. I would have breakfast with them and take them to school. After work, I would go straight back to the house and see them before bed. Once they were in bed, I would walk back to my flat, and just begin to despair. I was so worried about what we were doing to them. I was worried they would have the same issues that I did when my parents separated. But each time I thought deeply about everything, I realised our situation was very different to the one I gone through as a child. I was in their lives constantly, if not more than when we were together. I turned into Turbo Dad. I was trying to be more than everything. I was overcompensating, but I didn't care. If there was ever a time to overcompensate, this was it. And, looking back, and knowing what I know now, there's no such thing as overcompensation where separation is concerned. Giving an extra 10 or 100% reaps massive benefits to a precarious situation.

When I arrived home in the morning, my daughter Agatha would ask me where I had been. I didn't tell her everything straightaway, I felt she was too young to comprehend it. But after a month or two, she knew something was up, and we gave her a little bit more information on where I went. But because she was so wrapped in love and I was always there, it just wasn't a problem for her.

I was exhausted. I was doing a busy day in the hair salon and would try and get back to the family home as quickly as possible, finish up our bedtime routine with the kids and then back to the flat.

I began concentrating my efforts on my spiritual practice. I thought that if there was ever a time to dig deep and use this stuff, this was the time. The whole family was experiencing trauma, but I was also feeling an extraordinary sense of relief at the same time. It was strange. If I was out socialising or at a festival, I was able to forget, but then throughout the day I would I'd feel extreme moments of anguish. The loss of the family unit weighed heavily on me. I had known this moment was coming, but I had no idea how hard it was going to be. But time is a healer, and it did get easier once I accepted that the kids weren't affected. I was being honest with myself at all times, constantly monitoring their behaviour, trying to feel how they were feeling, and all I was getting was love, growth and prosperity and an eagerness in their eyes to experience life. I was never worried or alarmed that they were having some kind of negative reaction to what was happening. Nikki and I had discussed this a lot. We agreed that if there were signs of trauma or behavioural differences then we would rethink the plan. But the kids continued to grow in love. It was an extraordinary sight to see. And, I think Nikki and I can give ourselves a pat on the back for how we managed the situation. Whatever we did, we did it right. We were honest when necessary, we didn't stop disciplining our kids or teaching them lessons when needed, and we came together as one voice, perhaps not all the time, but enough. And, let's face it, what's not to love about being around two kids that you've made out of love?

After six months, we'd settled into our new routine. Things were tense between Nikki and me, but credit to us both, we were getting through it.

It was time I had my own place. Nikki let me sleep one night a week in the kids' room. We called it den night. I still do it today. We just camp out in one of the rooms. It's a brilliant legacy from that time. Financially, business was good, so I was able to get myself a one-bed flat. Finally, the kids could come over and stay with me. I was so happy. It felt like we were on an adventure. I was learning to cook, and we would have fun inventing games. It was just such a very special time. Money was scarce as I was paying the mortgage and paying the rent on the flat and everything else that comes with that. But I was happy. I was still having wonderful spiritual experiences throughout the day and evenings and I was still doing my weekly channelling evenings. I was in such a special place.

After a year in the flat, it was starting to feel small. It was only a one-bed place, so the kids would end up in my enormous super king bed. I had blown up beds for them on my bedroom floor and tried at some point in the night to lift them onto it, but it never worked. By the morning they were back again. Amazingly, Nikki got back into work, was bringing in a regular salary, and was happy to take on the mortgage. This was massive to me. I don't think I ever let her know what a huge thing this was and how life-changing it turned out to be. She was so giving. She never asked for any permanent maintenance money from me. She knew I had the kids as much as I could and that I would give them everything they needed, but to do that I had to live in some kind of comfort. So, one day I went online, and I saw this unbelievably cheap-looking property to rent. 'What was the catch?', I thought. Turns out the real catch was that it was in desperate need of redecoration. Brown carpets throughout and magnolia paint everywhere. I moved in on the 1st of December 2019. I immediately ripped the carpets up and sanded the floors with a huge drum sander, and got to work on redecorating. I've never sanded floors before, and I never want to do it again. They did look great though. It was worth the potential lung damage from all the sawdust I swallowed. It's a charming cottage, the kids love it here. It's within walking distance of school and Nikki's house. We're in this great little triangle.

The kids love having two properties, two Christmases, two of everything.

They're incredible and see more of each parent than they would if we were under one roof. It feels like we've created this utopian separated family set-up.

Nikki and I have a great schedule. We decided to share

the kids equally. It gave me a greater experience of fatherhood. I got to do things my way. Although it wasn't hugely dissimilar from Nikki's way, it was still my way. We both get a chance to influence the kids in the right way and on our own terms. It is really hard work, however. Being a single parent to curious creative kids is no small task. Nikki and I support each other where we can, and my place is within a kilometre of the family home, which is easy walking distance. Despite our occasional and natural frustrations with each other, we always make sure we do the best job we can. She's a fantastic mum, and I wouldn't change her for the world. She knows I'm a great dad too.

The separation was tough, although in hindsight I believe we're both glad we did it. The truth is we weren't right together. We had to find another way and we did. We've put the hard work in, put aside our feelings, and made sure we always put the kids first. If that happens then parents will always reap the rewards.

I think it goes wrong for kids when they see too much friction between parents. Subtle manipulation games and bad-mouthing would cause massive confusion and hurt for the kids. They can't ignore things. Most things parents do get observed by kids and logged in their brains. It's imperative that in the early days of separation, the mood and tempo are set. All the kids want is to feel part of a family unit, regardless of who's sleeping where. They want to feel, whether they are staying at mum's or dad's, that their other parent is not far away and will be with them soon. Both mum and dad should be in good spirits and communicating well with each other.

Both kids are flourishing and are exceptionally happy people. Their teachers comment on how emotionally intelligent they are. It's as though Nikki and I found a new paradigm for parenting. Having two households with different set-ups but the same foundations has made our kids very malleable and resilient. Their curiosity and creativity know no bounds.

We are in lockdown, and the pandemic is ripping through the planet. I'm in the bubble of our cottage with my kiddies and having a great time with them, although it's been exceptionally challenging at times. Homeschooling was difficult and when the kids aren't here, it has felt lonesome at times. Feeling and seeing people's anxieties and depression is tough. But we're all getting through it the best we can.

Hairdressers' stock has gone up and we are finally getting the recognition we deserve as the unwritten essential service, lol.

Life is tougher, but in my experience there's no growth without pain, and life just keeps changing, anyway,

We all know, planet Earth needed a break, and it looks like it's being forced to have one. Everyone's been slowed down and I've been made to take a long hard look in the mirror. Many of us would have asked ourselves what was important in our lives right now as we all spend time in isolation.

At the beginning of the lockdown, like many others around the world, I was on my knees in my living room, praying not to lose everything as it looked like my whole life was disappearing. But we're still here, providing for our families and living through this different kind of life.

I've been doing my sessions via Zoom. It was one of the best days of my life when I did my first live transmission, channelling from my bedroom. Everyone who had logged in had an extraordinary vibrational energetic experience. The energies that come through me speak of a grid of energy that covers the whole universe, so distance doesn't matter with energy transference.

I still have to pinch myself to remind me of this extra aspect of my life. I sometimes feel like an imposter. Why do I experience such things? But then I think, 'Why not me? Why can't anyone experience this wonderful aspect of life?'.

Ancient civilisations wrote about these phenomena for centuries.

The ancient Egyptians were very knowledgeable about chakras and unseen energies, as well as the power and capabilities of the pineal gland.

Almost every faith has recognised these human capabilities in one way or another over the centuries.

So, I think it's only right to share my experiences in this way. I definitely don't consider myself a holy person or particularly special. I just experience this majestic, almost unreal version of life. I fall short fairly regularly in my personal life like everyone else. But I pick myself up and I learn the lesson and make sure I do better next time. And if I don't, I keep trying.

I go over my day at the end of each day, seeing where I came up short, learning from that and rejoicing where I triumphed.

I had a very special evening recently, I was in the garden at about 9 pm, putting the rubbish out.

I looked up at the cloudy night and saw a huge light expand about 300 metres away. It shot across sideways, probably another few hundred metres and disappeared, as if moving at warp speed. It was far too close and big to be mistaken for a shooting star. It was incredible.

I have no idea what it was, but it was other worldly.

I went upstairs, hugged my kids, and told them I loved them. I didn't tell them what I saw until a few days later. I just wanted to process the experience before I started waxing lyrical about it. Luckily for me, UFOs are widely believed to be real. I've seen them before and they've been discussed in

US congress. Official footage has been recorded and navy and air force officials and British ministry of defence leaders, like Nick Pope, have discussed them at length. Governments around the world have set up agencies to monitor them.

Luis Elizondo was the former AATIP (advanced aerospace threat identification programme) boss at the Pentagon. This agency was set up to monitor UFOs. Of course, they treat them like a threat because little is known about them. He's gone on record, sharing a lot of what he knows. It's mind-blowing. He's since left the Pentagon to pursue this subject with a humane peaceful approach. I could go on listing the bona fide military officials who have seen and accepted we're being visited from the stars and beyond. The jury is still out on whether the visitors are folding space-time from vast distances or they're coming from another universe or dimension entirely. But one thing for sure is that they're visiting us.

I have no doubt in my mind we have visitors from afar coming to see us.

I have regular contact with them to this day. I've had too many experiences to think otherwise. They link with my consciousness and as with other non-physical angelic light beings, they somehow can transmit an energy to other people through me.

Bonkers as it is, it's happening. It has had a wonderful effect on my life and the people around me. It's not hurting anyone, only enhancing people and creaking open the doors of perception in their minds.

People sometimes ask me how they can experience such things.

All I know is how I came to have this in my life. This is why I wrote my story.

I knew nothing of unseen energies and chakras and aliens

or any other 'alternative' matters. They just weren't on my radar. All I know is, every time I got knocked down in life, I fought back hard with an open heart and a super-positive mindset. I didn't want to be beaten at any cost. I knew there was beauty in life even when it was dark. I took ownership of my shortcomings, working out how they arrived in me. Then, I counteracted them with a positive action that neutralized them.

If I was unsure about which action to take, I sought advice from someone that might know.

I did my research and used my common sense to find a way to be the best version of myself: physically, mentally and emotionally.

By doing this, the universe showed itself to be the most emphatically beautiful place possible. The nature of reality is a little clearer to me now. To my mind, we live in a responsive environment. What we put out, we get back. Cause and effect. Karma. Call it what you will. But from my experience, it's a path worth investigating. You just never know what you might find.